Piggy Foxy and the Sword of Revolution

Piggy Foxy and the Sword of Revolution

Bolshevik Self-Portraits

Edited by

Alexander Vatlin and Larisa Malashenko
Translated by Vadim A. Staklo

Foreword by Simon Sebag Montefiore

Yale University Press   New Haven & London

This volume has been prepared with the cooperation of the Russian State Archive of Social and Political History (RGASPI) of the State Archival Service of Russia in the framework of an agreement concluded between RGASPI and Yale University Press.

Designed by James J. Johnson and set in Sabon Roman types by Tseng Information Systems, Inc. Printed in Italy by EuroGrafica SpA.

Library of Congress Cataloging-in-Publication Data

Piggy foxy and the sword of
    revolution : Bolshevik self-
    portraits / edited by Alexander
    Vatlin and Larisa Malashenko ;
    translated by Vadim A. Staklo ;
    foreword by Simon Sebag
    Montefiore.
    p. cm. — (Annals of Communism)
    Includes index.
    ISBN-13: 978-0-300-10849-1
    (alk. paper)
    ISBN-10: 0-300-10849-4
    (alk. paper)

1. Soviet Union—Politics and
government—1917–1936—Caricatures
and cartoons. 2. Vsesoiuznaia
kommunisticheskaia partiia
(bol'shevikov)—Caricatures and
cartoons. 3. Politicians—Soviet
Union—Caricatures and cartoons.
I. Vatlin, A. IU. II. Malashenko,
Larisa. III. Title: Bolshevik
self-portraits. IV. Series.
DK268.4.P54 2006
947.08402′07–dc22

                        2006009070

A catalogue record for this book is available from the British Library.

The paper in this book meets the guidelines for permanence and durability of the Committee on Production Guidelines for Book Longevity of the Council on Library Resources.

10 9 8 7 6 5 4 3 2 1

Contents

PART TWO. Comrades and Problems

Foreword

SIMON SEBAG MONTEFIORE

The history of the Bolsheviks during the brutal turbulence of their long revolution, from the seizure of power in October 1917 through the Civil War and collectivization, up to the ritual cannibalism of the Great Terror, is as absurd as it is grim. Its tragedy is made for satire yet defies caricature, for its madness seems beyond humor. Hence the great value of this remarkable collection of cartoons, caricatures, and drawings is that both the artists and the subjects were Bolshevik magnates. Not only most of the subjects but most of the artists too were shot on Josef Stalin's orders during the Terror.

The caricatures are often outrageously, perversely funny. Indeed this book is highly comedic. But the laughter has an echo in the dungeons of Lubianka, and we can follow the foreboding and sadness and then the tragic bloodbath through these images. They are much more than just funny cartoons: they are golden assets for the historian, and I think, in the future, historians of Stalin and Stalinism will have to use this book.

They are of course part of the treasure chest formed by the Stalin and Politburo papers in the Russian State Archive of Social and Political History (RGASPI), formerly the Communist Party archive, in Moscow. The drawings and the archives themselves reveal a totally different picture of the Soviet leadership: beforehand, we were limited to monolithic histories of grim institutions—Politburo, Orgburo, Sovnarkom—filled with mustachioed men without biographies.

The RGASPI's wealth of archival material reveals the humanity of the leaders and, more important, how the entire regime worked on human terms: patrons and patronage, personal alliances and rivalries between characters and departments, fighting for power and, of course, for financial resources, were the essence of high politics in the Kremlin. We learn that Stalin himself did not emerge, fully formed after Lenin's death, as a steely figure of fear and reserve. Far from it, he built power not on fear but on personal relationships not only with his henchmen, such as Molotov or Kaganovich, but also with more formidable intellectual figures such as Kamenev, Bukharin, and Radek. The very top of the Bolshevik pyramid was a tiny group of fanatical Marxist-Leninists and tough managers, hardened by a long life of underground conspiracy and tsarist prison, bloodied in the savage killing of the Civil War, and later the war on the peasantry.

Stalin was the linchpin of these personal relationships, the patron of patrons, and the arbiter of departmental rivalries, but we must be careful not to write history backward. Until 1937, he was regarded as the toughest of the Bolshevik hard men, but he was still an old comrade: the archives reveal how intimately Stalin lived with the other Bolshevik leaders. He constantly dropped in on his neighbors and friends in their Kremlin apartments, suburban dachas, and Black Sea holiday villas, as witnessed by his many notes to friends like Klim Voroshilov, Vyacheslav Molotov, and Demian Bedny suggesting dinners or trips to the country as well as the discussion of political matters.

These grandees, with their wives and children, their country houses and family parties, presided over a state of repression and propaganda, a realm of misery and mass murder and prison camps. Yet the leaders could still tease and laugh at one another. The archives reveal the constant joshing and joking in Politburo meetings in which notes were constantly sent around the table and often Stalin himself took part. Only in 1937 did this collegial political world disappear forever.

All this is in these drawings, which helps us listen in on the tone of these talented but brutal leaders with their towering egos and ambitions. The cartoonists, leaders themselves like Nikolai Bukharin and Valery Mezhlauk, mock the vanities of their comrades in witty and sophisticated jokes and often obscene language and images: among so much political jargon and tough bargaining, we see hilarious images of castrations and genital dismemberments.

Here we can sense the idiosyncratic culture of high Bolshevism and its contradictions: the intellectual culture versus the rude working-class machismo; the strange system of repressive dictatorship mixed with the dying relics of party democracy; the matey comradeship of friendly equals in a party without a *Führerprinzip* alongside the growth of Stalin's personal tyranny; the cheerful rough bonhomie of old comrades undermined by the cheerless, po-faced ambition of Stalin's rising apparatchiks.

The story is told in these invaluable historic documents: they are often enjoyed by Stalin himself, who writes in his unmistakably emphatic scrawl: "Correct" or "To all members of the Plenum," because the drawings often serve his immediate political purposes. Many are especially revealing. The drawings by Bukharin and Yaroslavsky of Stalin himself (figs. 4–6) reveal him as friskily vigilant, grimly determined, and un-attractively long-nosed: they could have been drawn only by Soviet leaders before 1937, and it is no surprise they were drawn before 1930. Similarly, Trotsky appears as Stalin's comrades saw him—a preening Spanish troubadour (fig. 8). That was how Stalin saw him too.

The famous characters come across strongly: Yan Rudzutak's notorious laziness (fig. 25), Feliks Dzerzhinsky's almost religious fervor in his persecution of enemies (fig. 28), Bukharin's affable charm throughout, Voroshilov's mixture of vanity and fun. There are priceless portraits of Sergo Ordzhonikidze's dashing vigor, explosively pas-sionate Georgian temper, and relentless pursuit of Stalin's enemies (fig. 103). There is Anastas Mikoyan's dapper Caucasian glamour and Stalinist hardness. Both of these men were ruthless Stalinists, but Ordzhonikidze is ironically shown as a tsarist officer, Mikoyan as a Caucasian mountain warrior (fig. 157). Interestingly, Ordzhonikidze, the last big beast of the Bolshevik jungle, would be driven to suicide by Stalin in 1937, while the shrewd, feline Mikoyan turned out to be the ultimate Soviet survivor—a man who carried Lenin's coffin in 1924 and attended John F. Kennedy's funeral in 1963, finishing his career as chairman of the Presidium of the Supreme Soviet from 1964 to 1965.

Even the future NKVD head Lavrenty Beria appears at the 1937 plenum, still boss of Caucasia, using threats and denunciations to make his name and prove his potential to his patron, Stalin. As well as famous comrades, such as the blowhard leftist Grigory Zinoviev and his ally Lev Kamenev, the dreaded faces of less known Stalinist hatchet-men are fascinating too: the colorless Andrei Andreyev was one of the worst. The far from colorless but almost unhinged Lev Mekhlis, editor of *Pravda,* later political boss of the Red Army and killer of many of its officers, was so excessively Stalinist that even Stalin often mocked him for it. Mekhlis accumulated huge power as one of Stalin's private secretaries, and two others appear here: Ivan Tovstukha, until his death in 1935 the trusted guardian of Stalin's papers, and Amayak Nazaretian, who did not make it and was shot. In their place arose the grim Alexander Poskrebyshev (who does not appear in these pictures).

We know how vicious and serious were the ideological disputes among the leaders, but now we have learned too that many of the rows were not remotely ideological. They were personal fights and more often turf wars over resources and personnel. These documents show this clearly. The artists do not seem to foresee how grave these disputes would actually become: Stalin smacking the bare bottoms of Zinoviev and Kamenev may have been the worst that could be imagined at the time (fig. 104).

But Valery Mezhlauk's superb drawings in the 1930s are brilliant illustrations of the darkening sky: Stalin and his henchmen become increasingly furious about and frustrated by the economic problems and mechanical blunders, blaming their financial specialists. The experts were accused of corruption, double-dealing, and "wrecking." They were increasingly persecuted by Stalin and his brutal industrial managers such as Ordzhonikidze (fig. 152) and his friend, the former cobbler, Lazar Kaganovich (fig. 149).

The classic of the collection is where Mezhlauk mocks finance commissar Briukhanov, on 5 April 1930, and then Stalin adds his terrifying note about hanging him by his testicles: If they tear, then he is guilty; if they hold, he is innocent (fig. 135). Here is a preview of the witch-hunting style of the Great Terror of 1937, when death was random and people would die because of the look in their eyes. The cartoons illustrate how the failures of the regime, such as the constant train crashes, built up a pressure that only the Terror would release, and then in an orgy of bloodshed.

Mezhlauk skillfully shows the rise of the Soviet apparatchik in his series of drawings that mock the fat posterior and the bulging belly of this new breed. He satirizes the tedium of party conferences, the waiting in the anterooms: again, character is everything. There is still hilarity—as in the image of the veteran Georgian Bolshevik Felipe Makharadze urinating out his endlessly tedious speech (fig. 136).

There are many drawings that show the character of Mikhail Kalinin, an Old Bolshevik who had known Stalin since about 1901 and had succeeded Yakov Sverdlov in the ornamental position of head of state in 1919. He had moderate tendencies and an easygoing nature in a world of manic workaholics, but he was utterly incapable of exerting intelligence or will in any direction, bending to Stalin while trying to preserve his own good cheer. One of Mezhlauk's figures depicts him sending another famous personage, Marshal Semyon Budionny, to hurry up a boring speaker at a plenum (fig. 133). Budionny, with his flamboyant mustache, was the archetypal primitive Stalinist commander, a crony from Tsaritsyn in 1918, a swashbuckling hero of the regime for his command of the Red Cossacks in the Civil War. But as some of the cartoons reveal, he was far from appreciating the arrival of the mechanical age of fast-moving Panzer warfare, repeatedly denouncing tanks as inferior to his beloved horses (fig. 165).

The funniest of the collection is the telling 1935 duel between the talented cartoonists Bukharin (then enjoying a resurgence as *Izvestia* editor) and Mezhlauk about the latter's portrayal in the former's newspaper. Mezhlauk takes his vengeance by portraying Bukharin wielding a colossal erection; Bukharin replies by belittling his critic's equipment (figs. 137 and 138). Both were only a few short years from their downfall and execution. But Mezhlauk correctly observes the growing danger, the blood in the water. When Lev Kamenev, Lenin's old comrade and indeed Stalin's patron from Tiflis in the early 1900s, denounced himself at the Congress of the Victors in 1934, Mezhlauk draws him first disemboweling himself and then, tellingly, cutting off his own penis (figs. 163 and 164).

So we reach Mezhlauk's haunting and frankly outstanding artwork at the doom-laden, dark February 1937 plenum. There Stalin unleashed his attack dogs, such as the newly appointed NKVD commissar Nikolai Yezhov, his murderous and dwarfish impresario of the Terror. Mezhlauk no longer comments or jokes—he just observes and records, perhaps appreciating his own vulnerability. One senses his feeling of isolation from the disgusting proceedings and his realization that he no longer belongs in such ugly scenes. Mezhlauk was one of an extensive family of Bolshevik brothers, and he rose quite high, heading Gosplan but never reaching Politburo status. He clearly possessed a surprising sense of humor and perspective for a top Bolshevik.

Now, in 1937, he draws his old friend Bukharin as "Holy fool Bukharin Iscariotsky" (fig. 170). He sketches the dreadful dreary killer Andreyev chairing the witch-hunt at the plenum (fig. 173), and spots the rising star Beria, still Stalin's viceroy in the Caucasus but soon to emerge as NKVD commissar, Politburo member, gifted manager, father of the Soviet atom bomb, perverted sadist and rapist, and finally, the man who almost succeeded Stalin in 1953 before his own execution. Here Mezhlauk shows Beria denouncing the Old Bolsheviks of the Caucasus, all of whom would soon be slaughtered (fig. 179). Truly this was, as he noted, the dead end. It was to be Mezhlauk's too.

The collection has one more remarkable twist: the earlier drawings had been handed round the Politburo or Council of People's Commissars table and enjoyed by everyone, including Stalin. They were then given by Mezhlauk and Bukharin to the sentimental Voroshilov for his private collection, whence they made it into the archives. But the last set found here was obviously kept by Mezhlauk. When he was arrested months later in December 1937, the drawings were discovered in the usual search of his apartment and filed in his Lubianka dossier. He was shot in July 1938.

By that time, Nikolai Yezhov, commissar of the NKVD, was already in decline. By the end of the year, Beria had been brought to Moscow to destroy Yezhov and restore some orderly conduct to the business of mass murder. Reviewing his files, Beria found the drawings and sent them around the Politburo to the bigwig who would be most interested in that particular one, such as a picture of Andreyev that he addressed to its subject: "To Comrade Andreyev. Drawing by V Mezhlauk. L Beria." Molotov, Kaganovich, and the newly risen favorite, cultural expert and Leningrad boss Andrei Zhdanov, all received similarly lugubrious and macabre gifts. But Voroshilov got the most. Here is the ambitious and utterly ruthless new boy from the provinces, Beria, using the wit and artistry of a murdered man to win friends among the magnates of Moscow. Chilling indeed.

Most of the drawings ended up with Voroshilov. It is fitting that he became the keeper of this extraordinary collection, for Kliment Ye. Voroshilov personified many aspects of Stalin's regime. He was the ultimate Soviet grandee, a marshal, Politburo member, and people's commissar for defense (1925–40). Like Budionny, he was one of the regime's swashbuckling pinups. An Old Bolshevik metalworker who had known Stalin since 1906 (they shared a room at the Stockholm Congress), he made his name as a colorful and brave commander at Tsaritsyn in 1918, where Stalin met and liked so many of his military bunglers. Klim was good-looking and vain, flirtatious, kind, genial, and charming but was also a crude military commander and inept manager with a vicious temper, and a dangerous inferiority complex toward more talented generals. He was capable of ruthless brutality, and during the Terror he supervised the killing of around forty thousand Soviet officers, many of them his friends. Yet he had a taste for the arts, pretty women, and singing parties. He adored dancing and took fox-trot lessons to jazz music. Like most of Stalin's top deputies—Molotov, Mikoyan, Beria, Kaganovich, Andreyev—he survived the dictator and indeed served as head of state from 1953 to 1960, dying a beloved old hero.

Tellingly, Voroshilov continued to collect these drawings from his friends Bukharin and Mezhlauk even when he knew they would be shot, when he had signed their death warrants, when they were being tortured—and he kept the works long after their creators had been executed and buried in mass graves. That demonstrates how these caricatures are so much more than just cartoons sketched at boring Gosplan meetings. They unforgettably tell the tale of an entire epoch.

Acknowledgments

We would like to express our gratitude to Jonathan Brent, editorial director of Yale University Press, for publishing this unusual volume and for his active support and encouragement of this project at its every stage. We are grateful also to Vadim Staklo for his comments, edits, and additions, essential for a Western audience, and for his excellent translation of the book, which renders the peculiarities of the Russian language and the flavor of those cruel and extremely interesting times. We are particularly grateful to Phillip King, the highly professional manuscript editor, and our assistants Libby Kovach and Jaclyn Zubrzycki for painstaking work on preparing the text for publication. Our colleagues Oleg Khlevniuk, Larisa Rogovaia, Liudmila Kosheleva, Alexander Gribanov, and Vera Gribanova gave us invaluable advice and assistance while selecting images and preparing the text and the commentary.

Introduction

The former Central Communist Party archive (now the Russian State Archive of Social and Political History, or RGASPI) contains, in addition to its numerous manuscripts, a collection of drawings produced mainly by the leaders of the Bolshevik Party—using pens, pencils, and paintbrushes—during the interwar period. The sketches were made hurriedly, on notebook pages or the backs and margins of party records. The dates and inscriptions on the drawings indicate that they were mostly produced and shared during Politburo and government sessions, or during plenums of the Central Committee and party congresses. Often a drawing would turn into a sort of collective game: an initial sketch would acquire details and comments until eventually it was transformed into something like a modern cartoon. It is easy to recognize Stalin's blue pencil marks or the crude jokes of his entourage as they developed the idea of a caricature.

These "funny pictures" are an unexpected legacy from the creators of such a dismal era. What inspired this creative process? We can speculate endlessly, but we will never know for sure. Perhaps they wanted to illustrate dimensions of their political discussions that would otherwise be unacknowledged; perhaps they simply wanted to quell the boredom of daily sessions, to express their pent-up frustrations. Whatever the stimulus, these documents are a very special historic source that deserves the attention of scholars.

In contrast to more official discourse, these drawings reflect the spontaneous and sincere responses of the communist leaders to particular events: they contain much less of the falseness and sycophancy that strongly colored the behavior of the Soviet elite in the late 1930s. In a way, the drawings constitute a snapshot of the time, a testimony of immediate and honest witnesses. They shock the contemporary viewer with their crudeness and primitive nature. The drawings generated during Politburo meetings allow one to see the issues being discussed from a different perspective. Satirical language permitted the artists to say what was taboo in verbal discourse. Many caricatures made the Soviet leaders laugh even though they did not fit into official party ideology: it is hard to imagine these cartoons being published in the *Pravda* of the 1930s.

In this book we have selected the most vivid samples of the work of the high-ranking artists, those that preserve both the general tone of the time, when "socialism advanced on all fronts," and the specific ambiance inside Stalin's closest circle. Only a small part of the entire archival collection is included here, and publication is only the first step. Future researchers will complete the task of establishing the artists, commenting on the content, and tying the caricatures to specific events. Our understanding of the first two decades of Soviet history will be greatly enriched when scholars are able to study the Soviet leaders' attempts at artistic expression in addition to their official correspondence.

Humor of the Humorless Epoch

We venture to disagree with those who insist that caricatures and more general comic statements were impossible in the Soviet Union of this period given the existence of ideological censorship and a lack of political freedom. These drawings speak for themselves. They express a sense of humor that differs from both the official optimism of censor-approved satire and the alternative subculture of jokes and ditties. It was a specific humor developed for internal use, hidden for many decades between the covers of special files.

Readers who grew up in a free society will no doubt see this humor as timid, feeble, and deficient. It is common knowledge that comedy demystifies the world around us, breaking moral and ideological taboos, making us question established stereotypes. An authority that allows itself to be laughed at must have no doubts about its legitimacy. It was not an accident that in the early 1920s the only satiric magazines that existed in the USSR unquestioningly followed the party line. Notwithstanding all the "just cause" propaganda, the Bolsheviks had a strong inferiority complex.

But even as they deprived humor of its independence, the people at the helm still wanted to have some fun. Laughter helped to reduce the stress, to distract them at least briefly from tough problems; and that was important, considering the intense pressures within a system fueled solely by commands from above. Joking was both natural and necessary when long hours of Bolshevik leadership sessions grew stressful, and when tensions and hostile tempers needed release. Jokes were usually not recorded by stenographers, if the session was recorded at all, but their visual echo, in the form of cartoons and drawings, now belongs to history.

The great volume of cartoons in this archival collection makes it clear that this sort of art appealed to many members of Stalin's *nomenklatura*. It was a natural part of their lives, as ordinary as traditional hunting expeditions or group vacations to the Caucasus shore. It is indicative of the prevalence of this appeal that Leonid Brezhnev, a person not frequently associated with humor, once said during a meeting with cartoon artists: "By the by, in my younger years I played with very risky drawings. If I could show them to you, you'd die of laughter!"

One of the genre's oldest artists, Boris Yefimov, tells this story in his memoirs: "Regarding Stalin [I must say that], although he liked cartoons and always paid a lot of attention to them, he wouldn't allow any jokes about himself. . . . In 1925 I made a friendly drawing of him; it was returned to me with the short resolution: 'Not to be published!' " However, Stalin apparently made exceptions for his close circle—in this album, Stalin is both an author and a target of friendly caricatures.

The content of these drawings reflects not only many properties of the postrevolutionary period, but also the conflicted mentality of the new political elite. These men achieved absolute power over society, yet trembled in Stalin's presence. They were sure that history was on their side, yet could not cope with the simplest of problems. These drawings help us to grasp the group's character and understand more accurately the level of sophistication and education of the first generation of leaders of "socialist construction."

At this point two observations are necessary. First, it is interesting to note that the cartoons rarely address the problem of the Western world and foreign policy, even though official slogans demanded the fomenting of the proletarian revolution all over the world. Images of the fat capitalist or of German and Japanese aggressors appeared in the drawings only in 1937, and even then they were directly related to the unmasking of "enemies of the people" within the country. To a certain extent, this can be explained by the fact that the official propaganda published caricatures hostile to the outside world ad nauseam. But it is also possible that such indifference among higher-level leaders indicates their weariness of such political ballyhoo and their support for Stalin's policy of building socialism in one country. Second, the world represented in these drawings belongs entirely to men. The rude and sometimes obscene cartoons never concern half of humanity: women appear only as cleaning ladies or secretaries. The portrayal of someone as a "broad" was meant to be humiliating. Judging from both the available correspondence and these cartoons, the Bolshevik leaders' attitude toward women was conservative and paternalistic.

Cartoonists from the Bolshevik Olympus

It goes without saying that these cartoons do not belong to the category of great art, though their creators displayed, to varying degrees, some artistic skill. The drawings are more important as visual memoirs than as artistic achievements. Any memoir written by a person who was active and close to the top for a long time is guaranteed to provoke a great interest in the public, regardless of the literary merit of the text. The men represented in our book were not merely witnesses; they were the movers and shakers of the political process in the Soviet Union. The trends and dynamics of that process are not entirely transparent if we look only at written sources.

In order to fully appreciate these drawings as memoirs, it is important to know the main points in their creators' lives and careers. The first of the artists in talent and in political importance was Nikolai Ivanovich Bukharin. Born to a family of Moscow intelligentsia, he was educated at a gymnasium that provided some training in the fundamentals of art. Throughout his youth, even while engaged in revolutionary activity, the man who Lenin would later describe as the "darling of the party" developed his artistic skills: drawing was always one of his many hobbies. The harsh conditions of underground life and his nomadic existence in European exile made the preservation of Bukharin's early artistic productions impossible. The drawings of the postrevolutionary decades, on the other hand, survive in abundance. Bukharin preferred to work using the Indian ink technique, mastering the smallest details of his chosen subjects on the pages of his notebook. Unlike his colleagues, he rarely busied himself with caricatures of trivial moralizing mottos. He was more interested in nonpolitical topics, drawing landscapes, animals, and insects, studies in the style of cubism. His forte was the drawing of friendly cartoons depicting Politburo colleagues, sometimes with accompanying verses or pseudo-folk songs. The drawings are a testimony to Bukharin's sharp mind, social skills, curiosity, and particular ability to capture his subjects' whole personalities, not simply their weaknesses.

Valery Ivanovich Mezhlauk, the most prolific artist in our album, was not as famous as Bukharin. Like Bukharin, Mezhlauk had a gymnasium and college level education. He was also involved in revolutionary activity, and was a typical intellectual member of the Bolshevik Party. In the spring of 1918, Mezhlauk managed to rescue valuables from the State Bank of Ukraine and bring them to Moscow. Later he became a member of the Revolutionary Military Council in the famous Tenth Army that defended Tsaritsyn. There, Mezhlauk met Kliment Yefremovich Voroshilov. The two men remained friends until Mezhlauk's arrest on 1 December 1937. The peak of Mezhlauk's career was 1934, when he was appointed chairman of the State Planning Committee while also serving as Vyacheslav Molotov's deputy in the Council of People's Commissars.

In the early 1930s, Mezhlauk replaced Bukharin as the dominant artist in the Politburo. This change has symbolic significance; it reflects a new era of political thinking. Bukharin had preferred to draw lyrical landscapes; Mezhlauk was in favor of industrial scenes. If the former made cartoons with the intention of probing the psychology of his subjects, the latter was more interested in the function and position than the person. Mezhlauk's cartoons reflected current political events: an easily recognizable theme was usually combined with the locker room sense of humor that satisfied the tastes of the new elite.

In collections of Mezhlauk's artistic output, it is possible to distinguish series of drawings created during discussions of a specific problem or provoked by some big event. At first glance, the only common denominator appears to be the format of the notebook pages on which they were drawn, but a more careful study finds a common line of thought, a certain general attitude toward the issue and toward the personalities involved in the discussions. An entire series of cartoons describes the conflicts between various branches of the government during preparation of the state budget. As a member of the Presidium of the Supreme Council of the National Economy (VSNKh) since 1924, Mezhlauk was actively involved in those decisions. Especially interesting are the drawings related to the discussion on aviation. He made portraits not only of various people's commissars (*narkoms*), but also of directors of aviation plants and designers. Some of his last drawings were made at the Plenum of the Central Committee in February–March of 1937.

The biography of a third politician and artist, Moris Lvovich Belotsky, bears little resemblance to Mezhlauk's beyond a few limited similarities: both were friends of Voroshilov, who was the main fan of their satirical art, and both perished during the purges. Born to a poor Jewish family, Belotsky joined the Bolshevik Party in August 1918 and proceeded to make a brilliant career. He began as a political commissar in the Red Army. In 1923 he graduated from a military academy, serving first as a consul in Termez and later in the North Caucasian Territorial Committee. During the early stages of conflict between Stalin, Lev Kamenev, Grigory Zinoviev, and Lev Trotsky, Belotsky supported Trotsky, but he soon repented and returned under Voroshilov's protection. However, even the protection of Voroshilov was not enough: in 1937, Belotsky, serving as the first party secretary of Kirgizstan, was arrested for "connections with enemies of the people."

The first part of the album contains many portraits made by Yemelian Yaroslavsky, a devoted member of Stalin's team, who worked for many years in the Party Control Commission. His friendly cartoons appeared from time to time throughout the mid-1920s in *Rabochaia gazeta,* but he cautiously avoided offending anybody. In the early days of his career, in 1922 and 1923, he created a whole portrait gallery of his colleagues in the apparatus of the Central Committee of the party. There is nothing satirical about those portraits; they look rather like preparatory work for something large and serious that never quite came to fruition. The remaining works of Yaroslavsky are mostly oil paintings of neutral content.

Some of the drawings in this publication are of unknown origin. Sometimes they were the productions of talentless delegates who came from the provinces for party congresses and sent their pictures to a congress presidium or to party leaders. Many members of party and government leadership tried their hand at cartoons and drawings from time to time. In the archives there are works signed by Mikhail Tomsky, Yan Rudzutak, and Gleb Krzhizhanovsky. Even Stalin experimented with a pencil (fig. 63). His drawings are distinguished by their crude sense of humor, typical of the informality within the Politburo, and by their characteristically nervous style. Stalin's drafts often have doodles on the margins; their uncertain twitching lines differ enormously from his clear, strong handwriting, which can be observed in comments written on these same cartoons.

Structure and Principles of the Publication

The cartoons in this album capture the black-and-white world that surrounded these artists. This should be understood both literally and figuratively: most of the drawings were made in one color on white paper; they are also characterized by their extreme bluntness. The artists were certainly not given to nuance or shades of gray. A few political watercolors (including Mezhlauk's work in Part 2 of this album), are among the rare exceptions.

The first part of the album is titled "Gallery of Leaders." It contains portraits and friendly cartoon drawings of Bolshevik celebrities, secretaries of the Central Committee, officials of the central apparatus, chiefs of republics, and ministers. Both the images themselves and their inscriptions reflect the sympathies and antipathies of the Bolshevik leaders. They are an important comment on the political events of the 1920s and 1930s. The second part, "Comrades and Problems," contains multifigure caricatures depicting issues tackled by the leadership of the country. Through them, we can follow the discussion of problems and the decision-making processes of Soviet authorities at the highest level. These images are divided into several categories by theme: conflicts inside the party, the mechanics of Politburo sessions, and matters of economy. The final segment of the album contains artistic reports covering two especially tragic events in the history of the Bolshevik Party (VKP[b]) and the Soviet Union: the seventeenth congress of the party and the February–March 1937 Plenum of the Central Committee.

The main difficulty in preparing these drawings for publication is establishing the identity of their artists. These images were created neither for history nor for historians. They were variously exchanged or donated and then collected, and for that reason were generally kept not in the archives of their creators but in the archives of their collectors. The main collector of the drawings was Voroshilov. Aleksei Rykov, Karl Radek, and Felix Kohn collected images of themselves. To identify the creators of these drawings, we had to take into account their style and contents, along with other indirect evidence. Certainly, in several cases, our guesses and assumptions will be corrected by future researchers. A truly thorough investigation of this issue will necessitate an extensive analysis of all the artistic handwriting, and will require researchers to find and examine all the drawings and cartoons preserved in RGASPI and other Russian archives.

In many cases the published drawings are dated, often by the author, occasionally by the addressee of the cartoon. An analysis of the dates and times indicates that the authors worked on them during sessions of the top Soviet institutions. The dates on the drawings in our publication are as given by the author. We do not repeat the date while deciphering the inscription. If we have reconstructed the date, it is in brackets. Titles are as given on the drawings themselves; where there is none, we have added a brief descriptive name.

In addition to the data on the origin and date in the inscriptions accompanying each cartoon, we indicate the artist's technique and the work's archival data. We also decipher the inscriptions on the drawings. Although as a rule they were written by the artists, inscriptions in stylized fonts (as in block letters, etc.) cannot always be conclusively attributed. The reader should not be surprised that some artists, especially Valery Mezhlauk, commented on their own cartoons with different handwritings. According to his correspondence, Mezhlauk liked exercises in calligraphy. Occasionally, inscriptions were placed outside or on the other side of the drawing. In these cases they are reproduced only in our notes under the drawings. We have corrected grammatical mistakes in the original inscriptions without special notation.

To facilitate the examination of these images it was necessary, in the course of editing, to shrink or enlarge the documents, to take out the archival notations, and to neutralize the background of the paper used by the authors. Over the last three-quarters of a century, some of the paper leaves have become yellowed, and sometimes the drawings were found stained, wrinkled, and torn. When a drawing was made on stationery, we reproduce the image with the letterhead of the institution.

Our introductory notes for each segment of the album give a broader description of the pictures' context. They explain the position of the drawings in the first decades of Soviet history, and describe the greater and the more specific circumstances surrounding the political activity and decision making that provoked certain cartoons.

It is not our intention to comment extensively on each of the published documents; if it were, we would publish not an album but a monograph with illustrations. However, we hope that our audience will gain from this book an enriched understanding of interwar Soviet history and a deepened awareness of the Soviet elite of the time.

PART 1

Gallery of Leaders

It is important to remember that the following portraits of Soviet party and state leaders, made in the 1920s and 1930s, were created by amateurs, not professional artists, and were intended only for a narrow circle of comrades. Their historical value is much greater than their artistic quality. This part mostly contains the works of Nikolai Bukharin, Valery Mezhlauk, and Yemelian Yaroslavsky, who sketched these portraits of their colleagues in notebooks and on scrap paper during the working meetings and plenums of the highest party and state bodies.

As a rule, the amateur artists attempted to closely reproduce the appearance of their subjects. In order to make it easy to judge the success of these attempts, we have included photographs of the actual people next to their cartoon portraits. (For a handful of individuals, however, it has not been possible to obtain a photograph.) The caricatures are more interesting. They reflect the character of the subject, his attitude toward the issues on the agenda, and his place in the hierarchy of Bolshevik leadership. The artists were well aware that their work could cause anger and dissatisfaction. As a result, portraits of Stalin are never grotesque or even comical. But newer members of the Politburo were apparently much more open-minded about being lampooned.

The gallery of leaders opens with the most important Politburo members, followed by Central Committee workers, military figures, economists, bankers, and some prominent scientists and writers. We see together leaders of the internal opposition, Kamenev, Zinoviev, and Trotsky; chairmen of the government, such as Rykov and Molotov; and the temperamental Anastas Mikoyan and Sergo Ordzhonikidze.

Next come the portraits of the oppositionists (figs. 59–67), followed by those of high-ranking members of the Central Committee and workers in the Central Control

Commission (figs. 68–72) who played an important role in purging dissent and oppo-sition in the party. A frequent subject was Georgy L. Piatakov, the deputy people's commissar of heavy industry. His personal record had been marred by his friendship with Trotsky in the 1920s, which prevented this most talented economist from occu-pying the highest posts in the government. Another former member of the opposition, Karl Radek, also never became a political heavyweight. After Radek publicly recanted his oppositionist views, Stalin personally pardoned him and allowed him to work on foreign policy issues; even so, he was never elected a member of the Central Committee.

The gallery contains representations of four chairmen of the State Bank of the USSR (Piatakov, Nikolai G. Tumanov, Lev Ye. Mariasin, and Solomon L. Kruglikov), as well as of Nikolai P. Briukhanov, the people's commissar of finances until 1930 (fig. 76; Briukhanov also appears in the second part of the book, with Stalin's commen-tary, in fig. 135). Writings on the portraits of these Soviet finance workers (including those in Stalin's famous blue pencil) reveal the difficulty and danger of their work. Dur-ing the time of the forced industrialization and centralization of the monetary system, they had to satisfy institutional interests and simultaneously fulfill the Politburo's di-rectives to find additional resources for capital construction. They all became victims of Stalin's purges in 1936–37.

The next group of portraits depicts the heads of military and economic depart-ments. Some of them, like Vladimir A. Antonov-Ovseyenko, Nikolai Osinsky, and Gleb Krzhizhanovsky, wielded more influence than their posts would normally allow, due to their past contributions to the party. In all likelihood, only Krzhizhanovsky cor-responded to the image of the "Old Bolshevik": many of the other leaders were barely over forty, and they look like greenhorns in the drawings by their older colleagues.

Another set contains portraits of Central Committee apparatus workers sketched by Yemelian M. Yaroslavsky in 1923. The creator jokingly called it "the whole of the synkletos [Senate, in Greek], high brass, and the town elders," and noted that the gal-lery "still had an opening for the 'General' [Secretary] . . . (for the time being!)" Indeed, of the several dozen portraits, there are just a few of the original Politburo members. Most are images of little-known, low-ranking apparatchiks. Some of them, such as Amayak M. Nazaretian and Ivan P. Tovstukha, went on to have solid careers and even become famous; others quietly disappeared, victims of inner-party battles and under-handed intrigues.

A section of the album is dedicated to well-known figures in Soviet science and culture during the 1920s and 1930s (figs. 89–92). They came to be a focus of the amateur party artists as they ascended in rank and occupied positions of power. Nikolai D. Kondratiev was in charge of the Institute of Markets of the People's Commissariat of Finances, and David B. Riazanov was head of the Marx and Engels Institute (although their posts did not save them during the purges). The poet Demian Bedny and Arctic explorer Otto Shmidt were important propaganda icons, and thus frequent subjects of caricatures.

Finally, there are group portraits. Comments in the margins give us valuable information about the course of discussions about various issues among those in power, and about when the cartoons were created. One drawing in particular illustrates a typical problem: "organizing a syndicate for sales of poultry products in foreign markets"— that is, exporting eggs (fig. 93). In late 1927–early 1928, the interests of several powerful agencies collided over the issue of the centralization of exports. Archives retain records of heated battles fought over the course of many months. The decision to set up a syndicate, preapproved by the deputy heads of the Council of People's Commissars and the Labor and Defense Council on 15 March 1928, was not certified largely because of the opposition of N. A. Uglanov, head of the Moscow party organization and a future right deviationist. He was worried that the centralization of egg exports would exacerbate the already dire situation of food supplies in Moscow. The caricaturist portrayed him claiming that "Muscovites will gobble up the eggs on Easter." Finally, on 22 May 1928, the Politburo rejected the idea of a poultry-egg syndicate. This was probably the day of the creation of the group portrait of Tomsky, Mikoyan, and Uglanov.

The popularity of different Bolshevik leaders with the caricaturists depended on personal sympathies and antipathies, and on the willingness of potential subjects to take a joke. Piatakov, Mikhail I. Kalinin, Mikoyan, and Feliks E. Dzerzhinsky were preferred models for the artists. This collection includes only the most representative of the many caricatures and sketches of them. On the other hand, some well-known persons appear only in the second, topical part of the album. As for the artists themselves, Bukharin loved to mock himself, while Mezhlauk and Yaroslavsky shied away from self-portraits.

Bukharin was the most gifted artist of all. His caricatures, sketches, and portraits are original, very detailed, and demonstrate skill in various techniques. The dates on his drawings show that he worked on them in series, as inspiration struck him. On one day he created both a self-portrait and a portrait of Ordzhonikidze as a tsarist army officer (figs. 13 and 42). The timing of his drawings reflects the schedule of work in the state and party branches. Portraits of Dzerzhinsky and Kamenev are dated 25 June 1923; since there were no official Politburo sessions on that day, it is possible that Bukharin made them at one of the informal preparatory meetings. Soon after that, on 3 July, Dzerzhinsky spoke on the first four topics of the Politburo agenda. A caricature on Kamenev is tied to the discussion of the state budget on 14 June 1923 and the following days.

Bukharin did not hesitate to use grotesque images: a twiglike Karl Radek, shriveled by theoretical discussions by 1952 (a year he never lived to see; fig. 65); the keeper of party morale Aron Solts looking like an Athenian owl or a fairy-tail crow (fig. 68); an "animalistic" image of Zinoviev, dated 3 March 1926 (fig. 10). As president of the Executive Committee of the Communist International, Zinoviev was not a main speaker, but his spirited participation in discussions, coupled with his lionesque mane, seems to have evoked the image of a feral beast.

In one drawing Bukharin pictured himself as a "piggy foxy" (fig. 15). There are few piggish traits in the image, but quite a lot of foxiness: sharp nose and ears, bushy tail, and so on. We may never know what prompted Bukharin to depict himself like that, but, ironically, it accurately predicted his fate. In March 1938, Procurator General Andrei Vyshinsky thundered at the third show trial: "What about Bukharin, this vile mix of a fox and a swine, how did he behave in this regard? As it becomes a fox and a swine." What a tragic consonance!

Gallery of Leaders

Vladimir Ilyich Lenin (1870–1924) was one of the founders of the
Russian Social-Democratic Worker's Party (RSDRP). He was a member of
the Politburo in October 1917 and from 1919 to 1924. He was chairman of
the Council of People's Commissars (the government) of Soviet Russia from
October 1917, and chairman of the Defense Council from November 1918.

Fig. 1.
N. I. Bukharin, *V. I. Lenin.*
31 March 1927. Black ink.
Inscription: "V. I. Ulianov
(Lenin). For Comrade
Voroshilov." On the reverse:
"Bukharchik, 30 March
[19]27."
RGASPI, f. 74, op. 2, d. 168, l. 125.

Fig. 2.
N. I. Bukharin, *V. I. Lenin.*
15 June 1927. Pencil.
RGASPI, f. 74, op. 2, d. 168, l. 132.

Fig. 3.
Unknown artist, *V. I. Lenin.*
Pencil.
RGASPI, f. 74, op. 2, d. 168, l. 160.

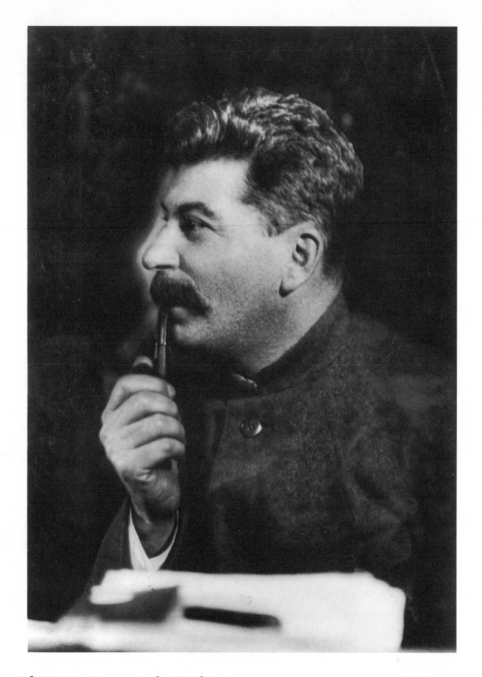

Iosif Vissarionovich Stalin (1879–1954). A party member from
1898, he was a member of the Politburo in October 1917 and from 1919 to
1953. He was general secretary of the party from 1922.

Fig. 5.
N. I. Bukharin, *I. V. Stalin.*
Pencil. Inscription on the
reverse: "Pb. [Politburo]
April 1929."
RGASPI, f. 74, op. 2, d. 169, l. 44.

Fig. 4.
N. I. Bukharin, *I. V. Stalin.*
20 February 1928. Black and
blue pencil.
RGASPI, f. 74, op. 2, d. 169, l. 11.

Fig. 6.
Ye. M. Yaroslavsky, *I. V.
Stalin.* [1923.] Blue pencil.
RGASPI, f. 89, op. 1, d. 158, l. 36.

Lev Borisovich Kamenev (1883–1936) was a party member from 1901 and a Politburo member in 1917 and 1919–25. From 1922 to 1926 he was deputy chairman of the Council of People's Commissars of the USSR, from 1924 to 1925 chairman of the Labor and Defense Council, and from 1923 to 1926 director of the Lenin Institute. He was condemned in the first show trial of the Great Purge and shot.

Fig. 7.
N. I. Bukharin, *L. B. Kamenev.* 25 June 1923. Black ink.
Inscription by the artist:

> *On Guard. Government Report.*
> Expenses are plenty, but . . . there is no income,
> And I wouldn't expect it soon.
> We have the "vision," "planned approach," and decrees . . .
> Money we don't have, and I don't know if we will.

At the bottom: "Drawn by N. I. Bukharin."

RGASPI, f. 74, op. 2, d. 168, l. 1.

Lev Davydovich Trotsky (1879–1940) joined the revolutionary movement in 1897 and was a member of the Politburo in October 1917 and 1919–26. From 1918 to 1925 he was people's commissar of the army and navy and chairman of the Revolutionary Military Council. He was expelled from the party in 1927 and exiled abroad in 1929. He was assassinated in Mexico.

Fig. 8.
V. I. Mezhlauk, *L. D. Trotsky.*
Pencil. Inscription by the artist:
" 'It happened in Spain' or
'Spanish Ahasuerus [the
Wandering Jew], wrapped in a
cloak, with a guitar under his
cape.' "
RGASPI, f. 74, op. 2, d. 170, l. 15.

Grigory Yevseyevich Zinoviev (1883–1936). A party member from 1901, he was a member of the Central Committee and the Politburo from 1921 to 1926, chairman of the Petrograd (Leningrad) Soviet from 1917 to 1926, and chairman of the Comintern Executive Committee from 1919 to 1926. He was found guilty in the first trial of the Great Purge in 1936 and executed.

Fig. 9.
N. I. Bukharin, *G. Zinoviev.*
25 June 1923. Black ink.
Inscription by the artist:
" 'Kulon' (a.k.a. leader of the
world proletariat)." The
meaning of "Kulon" is unclear.
RGASPI, f. 74, op. 2, d. 168, l. 2.

Fig. 10.
N. I. Bukharin, *G. Zinoviev.*
Black ink. Inscription by
Voroshilov: "Bukharin's
depiction of Zinoviev at the PB
[Politburo meeting]. 3 March
[19]26."
RGASPI, f. 74, op. 2, d. 168, l. 66.

Nikolai Ivanovich Bukharin (1888–1938) joined the Bolshevik Party in 1906 and was a member of its Central Committee from 1917 to 1934. From 1919 he was a candidate member and from 1924 to 1929 a full member of the Politburo and executive editor of *Pravda*. In 1929 he was accused of right deviation, although he was later reinstated, and he was executed in 1938 after a show trial.

Fig. 11.
UNKNOWN ARTIST, *N. I. Bukharin*. Black ink.
RGASPI, f. 74, op. 2, d. 168, l. 6.

Fig. 13.
N. I. BUKHARIN, *Self-portrait*.
17 February 1927. Black ink.
RGASPI, f. 74, op. 2, d. 168, l. 105.

Fig. 12.
V. I. MEZHLAUK, *N. I. Bukharin*. 26 January 1927. Black ink. On the reverse, inscription by the artist: "Mezhlauk. A grand maestro of the muddle-headed brotherhood."
RGASPI, f. 74, op. 2, d. 168, l. 90–90 rev.

Fig. 14.
YE. M. YAROSLAVSKY, *N. I. Bukharin*. Red and blue pencil.
RGASPI, f. 74, op. 2, d. 169, l. 39.

Fig. 15.
N. I. BUKHARIN, *Self-portrait*. Pencil. Inscription by the artist: "Piggy foxy in his (current) old age."
RGASPI, f. 329, op. 2, d. 11, l. 158.

Mikhail Ivanovich Kalinin (1857–1946). A party member from 1898, he was a member of the Central Committee from 1919, a candidate Politburo member from 1921, and a full member from 1926. From 1919 to 1938 he was chairman of the Russian and Soviet Central Executive Committees, and, from 1938 to 1946, chairman of the Presidium of the Supreme Soviet of the USSR.

Fig. 16.
Ye. M. Yaroslavsky, *M. I. Kalinin.* [1923.] Blue pencil. Inscription by the artist: "Hmm . . . I have lowered the RSFSR flag . . . Then what do I personify?"
RGASPI, f. 74, op. 2, d. 168, l. 17.

Fig. 17.
Unknown artist, *M. I. Kalinin.* 9 May 1929. Pencil.
RGASPI, f. 74, op. 2, d. 169, l. 48.

Fig. 18.
V. I. Mezhlauk, *M. I. Kalinin.* 25 April 1930. Black and red ink. Inscription by the artist: "Sovereign Kalinin: 'Those feudal scum! Pilfering and pulling the country apart! Plunderers!' "
RGASPI, f. 74, op. 2, d. 169, l. 86.

Fig. 19.
N. I. Bukharin, *M. I. Kalinin.* 25 April 1930. Black ink. Inscription by the artist: "Specialist in pinpricks."
RGASPI, f. 74, op. 2, d. 169, l. 89.

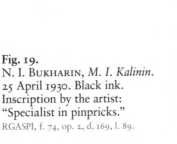

Vyacheslav Mikhailovich Molotov (1890–1986). A party member from 1906, he was a member of its Central Committee from 1921 to 1956. From 1921 he was a candidate member, and from 1926 to 1957 a full member of the Politburo. From 1921 to 1930, he was secretary of the Central Committee. From 1930 to 1941 he was chairman of the Council of People's Commissars of the USSR.

Fig. 20.
YE. M. YAROSLAVSKY, *V. M. Molotov.* 2 February 1934. Pencil.
RGASPI, f. 89, op. 1, d. 158, l. 14.

Fig. 21.
YE. M. YAROSLAVSKY, *V. M. Molotov.* [1923.] Blue pencil.
RGASPI, f. 89, op. 1, d. 158, l. 35.

Aleksei Ivanovich Rykov (1881–1938) joined the party in 1898. He was a member of the Central Committee from 1920 to 1934 and a Politburo member from 1922 to 1930. Rykov served as chairman of the Council of People's Commissars from 1924 to 1930, and was people's commissar of communications (mail and telegraph) from 1931 to 1936. He was convicted of treason and shot.

Fig. 22.
Ye. M. Yaroslavsky, *A. I. Rykov.* 20 February 1928. Blue and red pencil.

RGASPI, f. 74, op. 2, d. 169, l. 10.

Fig. 23.
V. I. Mezhlauk, *A. I. Rykov.* October 1927. Pencil. Inscription by the artist: "Dubito ergo sum" [I doubt therefore I am].

RGASPI, f. 74, op. 2, d. 169, l. 189.

Yan Ernestovich Rudzutak (1887–1938) joined the party in 1905. He was a candidate Politburo member from 1923 to 1926 and a full member from 1926 to 1932. He was secretary of the Central Committee from 1923 to 1924, head of the People's Commissariat of Transportation (NKPS) from 1924 to 1930, and deputy chairman of the Council of People's Commissars and the Labor and Defense Council from 1926 until his arrest in 1937 and subsequent execution.

Fig. 24.
V. I. Mezhlauk, *Ya. E. Rudzutak.* 3 February 1928. Black ink. Inscription by the artist: "Rudzutak defends the cost estimate of the NKPS."
RGASPI, f. 74, op. 2, d. 169, l. 8.

Fig. 25.
V. I. Mezhlauk, *Ya. E. Rudzutak.* Blue pencil. Inscription by the artist: "Missing person! Reward offered!"
RGASPI, f. 74, op. 2, d. 169, l. 111.

Mikhail Pavlovich Tomsky (1880–1936) joined the party in 1904.
He was a member of the Central Committee from 1919 to 1934 and a member of
the Politburo from 1922 to 1930. He was chairman of the All-Union Central Trade
Union Council (VTsSPS) from 1918. He was accused of right deviation in 1929 and
later committed suicide.

Fig. 26.
Ye. M. Yaroslavsky, *M. P. Tomsky.* [1923.] Pencil.
Inscription by the artist:
"VTsSPS."
RGASPI, f. 74, op. 2, d. 168, l. 14.

Fig. 27.
V. I. Mezhlauk, *M. P. Tomsky.* Pencil. Inscription by the artist:
"M. Tomsky before taking control over VTUZes." (This referred to
the Technical Establishment of Higher Education, a specialized
institution that trained engineers quickly, often through on-the-job
training in a working factory.) At the bottom: "V. Mezhlauk."
RGASPI, f. 74, op. 2, d. 169, l. 140.

Feliks Edmundovich Dzerzhinsky (1877–1926). A party member from 1895, he was founder of the first Soviet state security apparatus, known as the VChK, or Cheka, and served as its chairman from 1917 to 1922. (The Cheka was replaced in 1922 by the GPU, or State Political Administration, the forerunner of the NKVD and the KGB.) Dzerzhinsky was people's commissar of transportation from 1921 to 1924, and chairman of the Supreme Council of the National Economy from 1924.

Fig. 28.
N. I. BUKHARIN, *F. E. Dzerzhinsky.* 25 June 1923. Black ink. Inscription by the artist: "A symbion (a.k.a. John the Baptist from the GPU) (This one is no good)."
RGASPI, f. 74, op. 2, d. 168, l. 2.

Fig. 30.
V. I. MEZHLAUK, *F. E. Dzerzhinsky.* Pencil. Inscription by the artist: "F[eliks] Edm[undovich]. Sure, nowadays industry is not just having a life, it's in clover." Papers read: "Hand over to industry 150, 200, 100 million rubles."
RGASPI, f. 74, op. 2, d. 170, l. 104.

Fig. 29.
YE. M. YAROSLAVSKY, *F. E. Dzerzhinsky.* Pencil.
RGASPI, f. 74, op. 2, d. 168, l. 9.

Fig. 31.
N. I. BUKHARIN, *F. E. Dzerzhinsky.* 30 June 1925. Pencil. Inscription by the artist: "The punishing sword of the proletarian dictatorship, or Dzerzhinchik guarding the revolution." Inscription by Dzerzhinsky in upper left corner: "Missing here are Bukharin, Kalinin, and Sokolnikov with files dulling the 'sword.'"
RGASPI, f. 76, op. 2, d. 35, l. 4.

Andrei Andreyevich Andreyev (1895–1971). A party member from 1914, he was a member of the Central Committee from 1922 to 1961, and served as candidate member (1926–30) and full member of the Politburo (1932–52). In 1924–25 he was secretary of the Central Committee. He was later secretary of the Northern Caucasus territorial party committee (1927–30). From 1930 he was chairman of the Central Control Commission and deputy chairman of the Council of People's Commissars of the USSR.

Fig. 32.
Ye. M. Yaroslavsky, *A. A. Andreyev.* Pencil.
RGASPI, f. 74, op. 2, d. 168, l. 12.

Fig. 33.
Ye. M. Yaroslavsky, *A. A. Andreyev.* [1923.]
Blue and lilac pencil.
RGASPI, f. 74, op. 2, d. 168, l. 13.

Kliment Yefremovich Voroshilov (1881–1969). A party member from
1903, he was a member of the Central Committee from 1921, Politburo member
from 1926 to 1960, and people's commissar of defense from 1925 to 1940.

Fig. 35.
V. I. MEZHLAUK, *K. Ye.*
Voroshilov. Red pencil.
Inscription by the artist: "The
way they depict you in the
newspaper illustrations."
RGASPI, f. 74, op. 2, d. 170, l. 120.

Fig. 34.
N. I. BUKHARIN, *K. Ye. Voroshilov*. Pencil.
RGASPI, f. 74, op. 2, d. 168, l. 161.

Lazar Moiseyevich Kaganovich (1893–1991). A party member from
1911, he was a member of the Central Committee from 1924 to 1957, candidate
Politburo member from 1925 to 1930, and full Politburo member from 1930 to 1957.
He was secretary of the Central Committee in 1924–25 and 1928–39. In the 1930s he
headed several key commissariats.

Fig. 36.
YE. M. YAROSLAVSKY, *L. M. Kaganovich.* [1923.] Pencil. Inscription by the artist: "L. M. Kaganovich!"
RGASPI, f. 74, op. 2, d. 168, l. 31.

Fig. 37.
YE. M. YAROSLAVSKY, *L. M. Kaganovich.* Blue pencil.
RGASPI, f. 89, op. 1, d. 158, l. 42.

Sergei Mironovich Kirov (1886–1934) joined the party in 1904. He was a member of the Central Committee from 1923, a candidate member of the Politburo from 1926, and a full member from 1930. From 1926 to 1934 he was the first secretary of the Leningrad city and provincial party committees and the Northwestern bureau of the Central Committee. In 1934 he was elected secretary of the Central Committee. His assassination that year led to the unleashing of the Great Purge of 1936–38.

Fig. 38.
V. I. Mezhlauk, *S. M. Kirov.* 25 February 1931. Pencil. Inscription
by the artist: "Elastic Leningrad. Blow, Kirych, blow!" The balloon
represents the population of Leningrad, which officials were
inflating.

RGASPI, f. 74, op. 2, d. 169, l. 121.

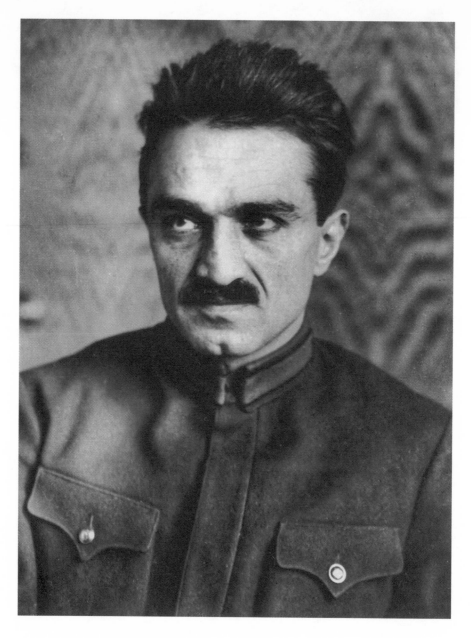

Anastas Ivanovich Mikoyan (1895–1978). A party member from 1915, he was candidate and full member of the Politburo from 1926 to 1966. He was people's commissar of domestic and foreign trade from 1926 to 1930, people's commissar of supplies from 1930 to 1934, and people's commissar of the food industry from 1934 to 1938.

Fig. 39.
N. I. Bukharin, *A. I. Mikoyan*.
20 October 1927. Pencil.
Inscription by the artist:
"Irrigation system."
RGASPI, f. 74, op. 2, d. 168, l. 143.

Fig. 41.
V. I. Mezhlauk, *A. I. Mikoyan*. Pencil. Inscription by the artist:
"Before the battle. 'What the hell is that blabber?!!' "
RGASPI, f. 669, op. 1, d. 14, l. 158.

Fig. 40.
V. I. Mezhlauk, *A. I. Mikoyan*.
Blue, red, and black pencil.
Inscription: "Mikoyan."
RGASPI, f. 74, op. 2, d. 169, l. 12.

Grigory Konstantinovich Ordzhonikidze (1886–1937), known as
Sergo, joined the party in 1903 and was a member of its Central Committee from
1921 to 1927. From 1926 he was a candidate member of the Politburo; he was a full
member from 1930. A member of the Central Control Commission from 1927 to
1934, he was also people's commissar of the Workers' and Peasants' Inspectorate
from 1926 to 1930. Ordzhonikidze became chairman of the Supreme Council of the
National Economy in 1930 and people's commissar of heavy industry in 1932. He
committed suicide during the purges.

Fig. 42.
N. I. BUKHARIN, *G. K. Ordzhonikidze.* 17 February 1927. Black ink. Inscription by the artist: "Sergo, if he was younger and served in the tsarist guard."

RGASPI, f. 74, op. 2, d. 168, l. 106.

Fig. 43.
V. I. MEZHLAUK, *G. K. Ordzhonikidze.* Black and red pencil. Inscription by the artist: "A rare quiet minute (before the battle)."

RGASPI, f. 74, op. 2, d. 170, l. 125.

Valerian Vladimirovich Kuibyshev (1888–1935) joined the party in 1904 and was a member of its Politburo from 1927. He was chairman of the Central Control Commission from 1923 to 1927, chairman of the Supreme Council of the National Economy (VSNKh) from 1926 to 1930, and chairman of the State Planning Committee.

Fig. 44.
Ye. M. Yaroslavsky, *V. V. Kuibyshev.* [1923.] Blue pencil.
RGASPI, f. 74, op. 2, d. 168, l. 8.

Fig. 45.
V. I. Mezhlauk, *V. V. Kuibyshev.* 26 January 1927. Pencil.
Inscription by the artist in Greek and Russian: "Verily, I say unto
you." On the reverse: "Chairman of the VSNKh Kuibyshev giving a
speech. 26 January [19]27. Mezhlauk."
RGASPI, f. 74, op. 2, d. 168, l. 91.

Vlas Yakovlevich Chubar (1891–1939) joined the Bolshevik Party in 1917 and was member of the Politburo from 1935 to 1938. From 1923 to 1934 he was chairman of the Council of People's Commissars of Ukraine. He was deputy chairman of the Council of People's Commissars and the Labor and Defense Council of the USSR from 1934 to 1937. He was people's commissar of finances from 1937 until his arrest and subsequent execution.

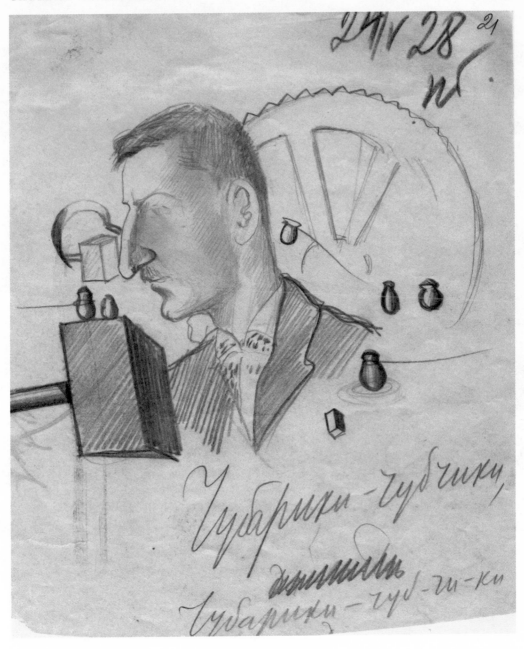

Fig. 46.
N. I. Bukharin, *V. Ya. Chubar.* 24 May 1928. Pencil. Inscription by the artist: "Chubariki-chubchiki,
Chubariki-chub-chi-ki" (a popular ditty, consonant with Chubar's name).

RGASPI, f. 74, op. 2, d. 169, l. 21.

Stanislav Vikentievich Kosior (1889–1939). A party member from 1907, he was a candidate Politburo member from 1927 and full member from 1930. From 1925 to 1928 he was secretary of the Central Committee, and from 1928 to 1938 he was the first secretary of the Central Committee of the Ukrainian Communist Party. He was deputy chairman of the Council of People's Commissars from January 1938, until his arrest and execution.

Мал золотник,
да дорог.

Fig. 47.
V. I. Mezhlauk, *S. V. Kosior.*
9 February 1927. Blue and red
pencil. Inscription by the artist:
"Good things come in small
packages." On the reverse,
inscription by Voroshilov:
"S. Kosior by Mezhlauk."
RGASPI, f. 74, op. 2, d. 168, l. 182–182 rev.

Fig. 48.
Ye. M. Yaroslavsky, *S. V.
Kosior.* Blue and red pencil.
RGASPI, f. 74, op. 2, d. 169, l. 9.

Fig. 49.
Unknown artist, *S. V. Kosior.*
Blue pencil.
RGASPI, f. 74, op. 2, d. 169, l. 35.

S. I. Syrtsov (1893–1939) joined the party in 1913; he was a candidate and full member of the Central Committee from 1924 to 1930, and a candidate Politburo member from 1929 to 1930. Head of the Central Committee department from 1921 to 1926, he was chairman of the Council of People's Commissars of the Russian Federation. He worked as an economic manager from 1931 until his arrest.

Fig. 50.
V. I. MEZHLAUK, *Syrtsov and Kosior*. Pencil. Inscription by the
artist: "Kosior to Syrtsov: 'Step up on the pulpit, I can't see you.'"
RGASPI, f. 74, op. 2, d. 168, l. 20.

Andrei Sergeyevich Bubnov (1883–1938). A party member from 1903, he was head of the agitation and propaganda department of the Central Committee from 1922 to 1924, head of the political administration of the Red Army, member of the Revolutionary Military Council from 1924 to 1929, and secretary of the Central Committee in 1925. From 1929 to 1937 he was people's commissar of education. He was arrested and executed during the purges.

Fig. 51.
Ye. M. Yaroslavsky, *A. S. Bubnov.* 25 November 1924. Pencil.

RGASPI, f. 89, op. 1, d. 158, l. 26.

Fig. 52.
Ye. M. Yaroslavsky, *A. S. Bubnov.* [1923.] Pencil. Inscription by the artist: "Lef Bub - - - -"

RGASPI, f. 74, op. 2, d. 164, l. 37.

Gleb Maksimilianovich Krzhizhanovsky (1872–1959). A party
member from 1893 and a member of the Central Committee from 1924 to 1939,
he was vice president of the Soviet Academy of Sciences from 1929 to 1939 and
chairman of the Chief Administration of Energy Services and Organizations
(Glavenergo) from 1930 to 1932. From 1930 he was head of the Institute of Energy of
the Academy of Sciences and deputy chairman of the State Planning Committee.

Fig. 53.
V. I. MEZHLAUK, *G. M. Krzhizhanovsky*. Black and red pencil. Inscription by the artist: "I already can see the Moscow of the future, inspired by the new creativity."
RGASPI, f. 74, op. 2, d. 170, l. 109.

Fig. 54.
V. I. MEZHLAUK, *G. M. Krzhizhanovsky*. Pencil. Inscription by the artist: "G.M.K. 'We are going to write a book [titled] Problemology.'"
RGASPI, f. 669, op. 1, d. 14, l. 191.

Nadezhda Konstantinovna Krupskaia (1869–1939), Lenin's wife. She joined the party in 1898 and was a member of its Central Control Committee from 1924 and the Central Committee from 1927. In 1929 she became deputy people's commissar of education.

Fig. 55.
V. I. Mezhlauk, *N. K. Krupskaia*. 1 June 1933. Black and red pencil. Inscriptions: "member of the C[entral] C[ontrol] C[ommittee]. V I M[ezhlauk]." "P[olit] B[ureau]"
RGASPI, f. 74, op. 2, d. 169, l. 179.

Maksim Maksimovich Litvinov (1876–1951) was a party member from 1898, and a member of the Central Committee from 1934 to 1941. He was deputy and later people's commissar of foreign affairs from 1921 to 1939.

Fig. 57.
YE. M. YAROSLAVSKY, *M. M. Litvinov*. Pencil. Inscriptions: "I could subsist on a crumb of bread. To the protocol of the session of 8 April [19]24." "The thing is: there is not a crumb."
RGASPI, f. 89, op. 1, d. 158, l. 18.

Fig. 56.
V. I. MEZHLAUK, *M. M. Litvinov*. Pencil. Inscription by the artist: "NKID [People's Commissariat of Foreign Affairs] listening to the plan for financing the industry. 31 January 1928."
RGASPI, f. 74, op. 2, d. 169, l. 5.

Fig. 58.
YE. M. YAROSLAVSKY, *M. M. Litvinov*. Pencil.
RGASPI, f. 89, op. 1, d. 158, l. 19.

Georgy Leonidovich Piatakov (1890–1937) was a member of the
Bolshevik Party from 1910, and a member of the Central Committee in 1923–27 and
1930–36. In 1929–30 he was chairman of the board of the State Bank of the USSR;
he was a member of the Presidium of the Supreme Council of the National Economy
from 1930 to 1931, and deputy people's commissar of heavy industry. He was
sentenced to death following the second show trial and executed in January 1937.

Fig. 59.
V. I. Mezhlauk, *G. L. Piatakov*. 8 June 1932. Pencil. Inscription by the artist: "Yuri Pyatachenko."

RGASPI, f. 74, op. 2, d. 169, l. 147.

Fig. 61.
V. I. Mezhlauk, *G. L. Piatakov*. 8 May 1935. Pencil. Inscription by the artist: "Greedy eyes, itchy palm." Inscription: "To STO" [possibly an abbreviation for Labor and Defense Council].

RGASPI, f. 74, op. 2, d. 169, l. 170.

Fig. 63.
I. V. Stalin, *G. L. Piatakov*. Pencil. Inscription by the artist: "Piatachenko. Koba pinxit [painted by Koba]." Inscription: "To Lunacharsky. A sample of oriental art." ("Koba" was Stalin's revolutionary pseudonym and an appellation used by his close associates.)

RGASPI, f. 558, op. 2, d. 520, l. 10.

Fig. 60.
Unknown artist, *G. L. Piatakov*. April 1933. Red pencil. Inscription: "Yu. L. P. by the end of session."

RGASPI, f. 74, op. 2, d. 169, l. 164.

Fig. 62.
V. I. Mezhlauk, *G. L. Piatakov*. Black and red pencil. Inscription by the artist: "Katzenjammer [hangover, in German], or the D[efense] C[ommission] elegy."

RGASPI, f. 74, op. 2, d. 170, l. 126.

Karl Berngardovich Radek (born Sobelson, 1885–1939) joined the party in 1903. In the early 1920s he was secretary of the Executive Committee of the Communist International. From 1925 to 1927 he was rector of the Communist University for Toilers of the East (KUTV) and head of the Bureau for International Information of the Central Committee. He was arrested and sentenced to ten years in prison, where he died.

Fig. 64.
N. I. Bukharin, *K. B. Radek*. Black ink. Inscription by the artist: "Lord Radek, earl of Sobelson. [In German:] On the report on the lords. Not for Falk." (Falk was a popular German publisher of tourist guides.)
RGASPI, f. 326, op. 2, d. 19, l. 27.

Fig. 65.
N. I. Bukharin, *K. B. Radek*. Black ink. Inscription by the artist (in German): "Radek in the year 1952."
RGASPI, f. 326, op. 2, d. 19, l. 29.

Ivar Tenisovich Smilga (1892–1937). A party member from 1907, he was a
member of its Central Committee from 1925 to 1927. Smilga was deputy chairman
of the State Planning Committee in 1924–25, and rector of the Plekhanov Institute of
Economy from 1926 to 1930. He died in the purges.

Fig. 66.
Unknown artist, *I. T. Smilga*. Black and red pencil. Inscription by Bukharin: "If Trotsky won't marry me, Chicherin will." Probably refers to the discussion about where to dispatch the Old Bolshevik Smilga, to the defense ministry, where Trotsky was people's commissar, or the foreign ministry under Georgy V. Chicherin.
RGASPI, f. 89, op. 1, d. 158, l. 5.

Fig. 67.
Unknown artist, *I. T. Smilga*.
Blue and black pencil.
RGASPI, f. 326, op. 2, d. 19, l. 20.

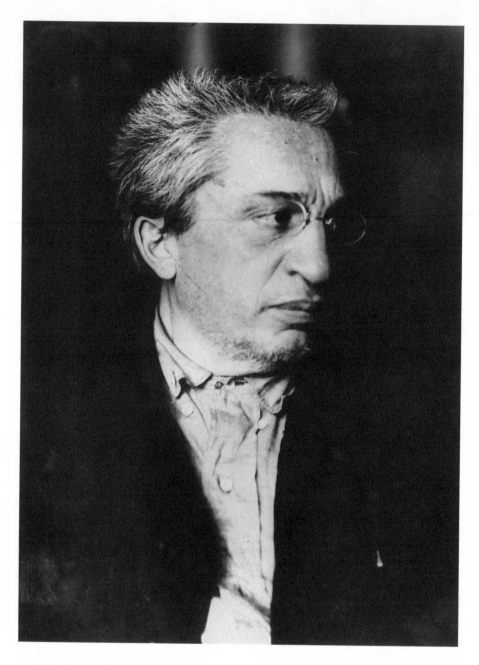

Aron Aleksandrovich Solts (1872–1945). A party member from 1898, he was a member of the Central Control Commission from 1923 to 1938 and chairman of the judiciary collegium for criminal cases of the Supreme Court of the Russian Federation.

Fig. 69.
N. I. BUKHARIN, *A. A. Solts*. 15 June 1933. Pencil. Inscription by the artist: "Bukharin, 15 June [19]33." On the reverse: "Solts, A. A."
RGASPI, f. 74, op. 2, d. 169, l. 180–180 rev.

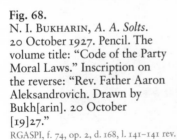

Fig. 68.
N. I. BUKHARIN, *A. A. Solts*. 20 October 1927. Pencil. The volume title: "Code of the Party Moral Laws." Inscription on the reverse: "Rev. Father Aaron Aleksandrovich. Drawn by Bukh[arin]. 20 October [19]27."
RGASPI, f. 74, op. 2, d. 168, l. 141–141 rev.

Fig. 70.
YE. M. YAROSLAVSKY, *A. A. Solts*. Blue pencil. Inscription by the artist: "C[entral] C[ontrol] C[ommission]."
RGASPI, f. 89, op. 1, d. 158, l. 41.

Matvei Fyodorovich Shkiriatov (1883–1954). A party member from
1906, he worked in the Central Committee apparatus from 1921 and was a member
and secretary of the Central Control Commission from 1923.

Fig. 71.
YE. M. YAROSLAVSKY, *M. F. Shkiriatov.* [1923.] Blue and lilac pencil. Inscription by the artist:
"1/100. See [Vladimir] Ilyich [Lenin's] article on the W[orkers' and] P[easants'] Insp[ectorate]."
(Refers to Lenin's article "How We Should Reorganize the Workers' and Peasants' Inspectorate,"
from 23 January 1923, in which he proposed electing an additional one hundred workers to
the Central Control Commission and reducing the number of inspectorate members.)
RGASPI, f. 74, op. 2, d. 168, l. 24.

Yemelian Mikhailovich Yaroslavsky (1878–1943). A party member from 1898, he was secretary of the Central Committee in 1921–22. From 1923 to 1934 he worked in the Central Control Commission and was on the editorial boards of the newspaper *Pravda* and the journal *Bolshevik*.

Fig. 72.
YE. M. YAROSLAVSKY, *Self-portrait.* [1923.] Blue and lilac pencil. Inscription by the artist: "Yemelian the Godless." (Sometimes referred to as a "Soviet priest," Yaroslavsky was the organizer of antireligious campaigns in Soviet Russia.)
RGASPI, f. 74, op. 2, d. 168, l. 16.

Lev Yefimovich Mariasin (1894–1937) joined the party in 1915 and was deputy department head of the Central Committee from 1927 to 1928, and chairman of the board of the State Bank of the USSR from 1934 to 1936. He died in the purges.

Fig. 73.
V. I. MEZHLAUK, *L. Ye. Mariasin*. 5 January 1935. Pencil.
Inscription by the artist: "C[omrade] Mariasin: 'A certificate? One moment . . . Oh, damn, looks like, instead of a pocket, I put it in a hole.'" Inscription at the top by Stalin: "Correct!" On the reverse, inscription by the artist: "For K. Ye. Voroshilov."
RGASPI, f. 74, op. 2, d. 170, l. 35.

Solomon Lazarevich Kruglikov (1899–1938). A party member from 1918, he was deputy head and head of the prices sector of the People's Commissariat of Heavy Industry from 1933 to 1936, and served as chairman of the board of the State Bank and deputy people's commissar of finances from 1936 to 1937, until his arrest and death in the purges.

Fig. 74.
V. I. Mezhlauk, *S. L. Kruglikov.* 20 June 1931.
Pencil. Inscription by the artist: "C[omrade] Kruglikov
reports on raising the prices for coal: 'You, comrade,
will pay just a tad more, a mere 500 thousand.'"
RGASPI, f. 74, op. 2, d. 169, l. 128.

Nikolai Gavrilovich Tumanov (1887–1936) joined the party in 1917. He was chairman of the board of the State Bank from 1924 to 1926, Soviet trade representative in France from 1928 to 1931, member of the Presidium of the Supreme Council of the National Economy of the USSR from 1931 to 1932, and chairman of the board and CEO of the Industrial Bank from 1932 to 1936. He died in the purge.

Fig. 75.
V. I. MEZHLAUK, N. G.
Tumanov. Blue pencil.
Inscription by the artist: "State
banker in August [19]25."
RGASPI, f. 669, op. 1, d. 14, l. 160.

Nikolai Pavlovich Briukhanov (1878–1938). A party member from 1902, he was people's commissar of food supplies from 1923 to 1926, and people's commissar of finances from 1926 to 1930. He was arrested and shot in 1938.

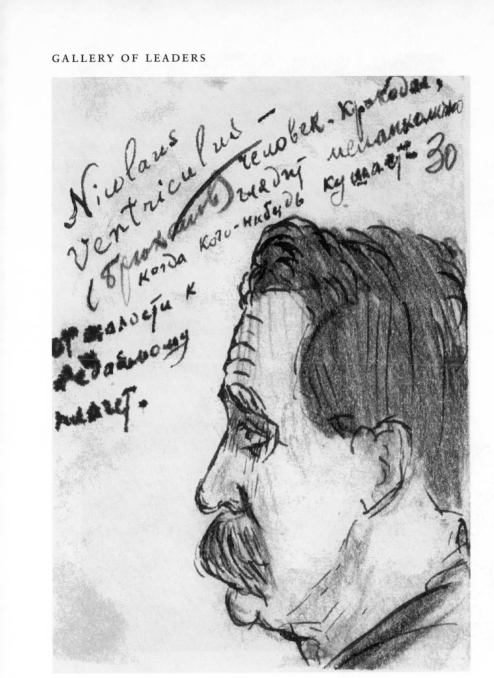

Fig. 76.
UNKNOWN ARTIST, *N. P. Briukhanov.* Pencil and blue ink.
Inscription: "*Nicolaus Ventriculus* (Briukhanov)—a crocodile man,
stares melancholically as he eats somebody up, crying with pity for
the one being consumed."
RGASPI, f. 74, op. 2, d. 169, l. 30.

Georgy Ippolitivich Lomov (born Oppokov, 1888–1938) joined the party in 1903. He was chairman of the board of the Donetsk coal company (Donugol) and member of the Politburo of the Communist Party of Ukraine from 1926 to 1929, and deputy chairman of the State Planning Committee of the USSR from 1931 to 1933. He was arrested in 1937 and sentenced to be shot.

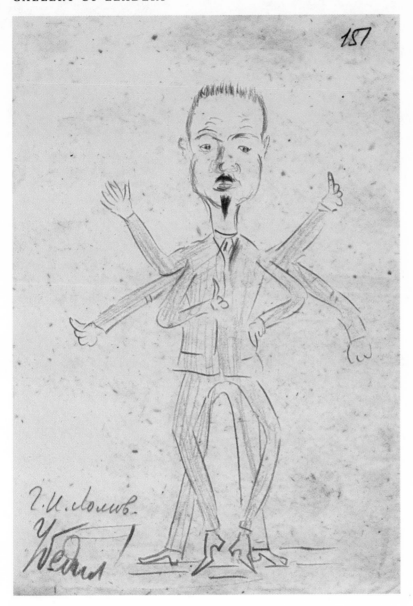

Fig. 77.
V. I. Mezhlauk, *G. I. Lomov*. Lilac pencil.
Inscriptions: "Convinced [me]!" "G. I. Lomov."
RGASPI, f. 74, op. 2, d. 170, l. 151.

A. I. Gurevich (1896–1937) joined the party in 1916 and was a member of its Central Control Commission from 1927 to 1934. He was a member of the Presidium of the Supreme Council of the National Economy from 1930 to 1931. From 1932 until his arrest and execution in 1937, he was deputy people's commissar of heavy industry and head of the Chief Administration of the Metallurgical Industry.

Fig. 78.
V. I. Mezhlauk, *A. I. Gurevich*. Black ink. Inscription by the artist:
"Gurevich: 'I spent every night for a whole month talking to a person
who gave his [expert] opinion; now he is giving his testimony.'"
RGASPI, f. 74, op. 2, d. 169, l. 115.

Nikolai Osinsky (born Valerian Valerianovich Obolensky, 1887–1938).
A party member from 1907, he was a candidate Central Committee member in
1922 and from 1925 to 1937. He was head of the Central Statistical Administration
from 1925 to 1928, and deputy chairman of the Supreme Council of the National
Economy and deputy chairman of the State Planning Committee. He was sentenced
to death and shot in 1938.

Fig. 79.
V. I. Mezhlauk, N. *Osinsky*. Pencil. Inscription by the artist: "*Osinsky*: 'My esteemed opponents say that I am a counterrevolutionary. It is insulting and incorrect. Thus I am saying that they are counterrevolutionaries—it is polite and correct.'"
RGASPI, f. 74, op. 2, d. 170, l. 60.

Vasily V. Shmidt (1886–1938) joined the party in 1905 and was a candidate Central Committee member from 1924 to 1934. He was a full member from 1925 to 1930. He was a member of the Presidium and secretary of the All-Russian Central Trade Union Council from 1918, and served until 1928 as the people's commissar of labor. From 1928 to 1930 he was deputy chairman of the Council of People's Commissars and the Labor and Defense Council. He was arrested in 1937 and later executed.

Fig. 80.
YE. M. YAROSLAVSKY, *V. V. Shmidt*. [1923.] Blue pencil.
RGASPI, f. 74, op. 2, d. 168, l. 18.

Robert Petrovich Eideman (1895–1937) was head and commissar of the Frunze Military Academy from 1924 to 1932. From 1932 until his arrest in 1937 he was chairman of the Osoaviakhim (The All-Union Society for the Support of Defense, Air Force, and the Chemical Industry).

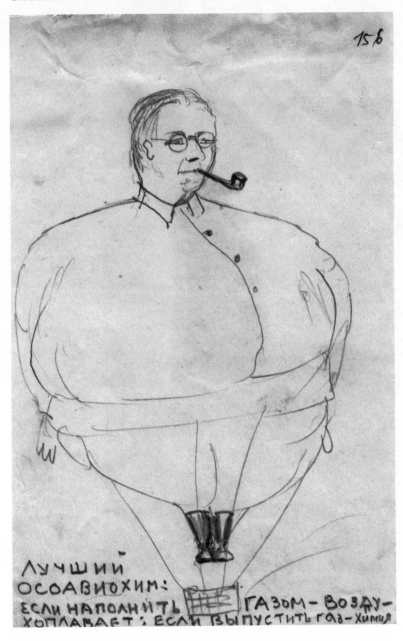

Fig. 81.
V. I. Mezhlauk, *R. P. Eideman.* Pencil. Inscription by the artist:
"The best Osoaviakhim: fill it with gas, and it floats; release gas—
then it's chemistry."
RGASPI, f. 74, op. 2, d. 169, l. 156.

Mikhail Mikhailovich Lashevich (1884–1928) joined the party in
1901 and was a candidate Central Committee member from 1925 to 1927. In 1925 he
was deputy people's commissar for the army and the navy, deputy chairman of the
Revolutionary Military Council, and member of the Presidium of the Supreme
Council of the National Economy. From 1926 to 1928 he was deputy chairman of
the Chinese-Eastern Railway board.

Fig. 82.
V. I. MEZHLAUK, *M. M. Lashevich*. Pencil. Inscription: "Who the hell do they think they are?" On the reverse: "For M. M. Lashevich."
RGASPI, f. 669, op. 1, d. 14, l. 179.

Vladimir Aleksandrovich Antonov-Ovseyenko (1883–1938)
joined the party in 1903. He was head of the political administration of the
Revolutionary Military Council of the USSR from 1922 to 1924, a diplomat from
1924 to 1934, procurator of the Russian Federation in 1934–36, and people's
commissar of justice in 1937 until his arrest and subsequent execution.

Fig. 83.
Ye. M. Yaroslavsky, *V. A. Antonov-Ovseyenko*.
Pencil.
RGASPI, f. 89, op. 1, d. 158, l. 7.

Sergei Sergeyevich Kamenev (1881–1936) joined the party in 1930. From 1927 to 1934 he was deputy people's commissar of the army and the navy and deputy chairman of the Revolutionary Military Council. From 1934 he was head of the Anti-Aircraft Administration of the Red Army.

Fig. 84.
UNKNOWN ARTIST, *S. S. Kamenev.* Violet ink. Inscription: "S. S. Kamenev:
'I should build another highway!!?? You must be crazy!!!'"
RGASPI, f. 74, op. 2, d. 169, l. 185.

Ivan Pavlovich Tovstukha (1889–1935) joined the party in 1913 and was a candidate Central Committee member from 1934. During 1921–24 and 1926–30 he worked in the Central Committee apparatus. After 1922 he was second assistant to the general secretary of the Central Committee, and deputy head of the Bureau of the Secretariat of the Central Committee.

Fig. 85.
YE. M. YAROSLAVSKY, *I. P. Tovstukha*. [1923.] Pencil. Inscription:
"Assistant deputy head, etc. Tovstukha (?)."
RGASPI, f. 74, op. 2, d. 168, l. 47.

V. N. Vasilievsky (1893–1957). A party member from 1912, he was deputy secretary of the Central Committee from 1921 to 1925 and deputy head of the Central Committee's press department from 1925 to 1927. After 1929 he was a member of the boards of the newspapers *Izvestia* and *Pravda* and worked in the committee for the arts of the Council of People's Commissars.

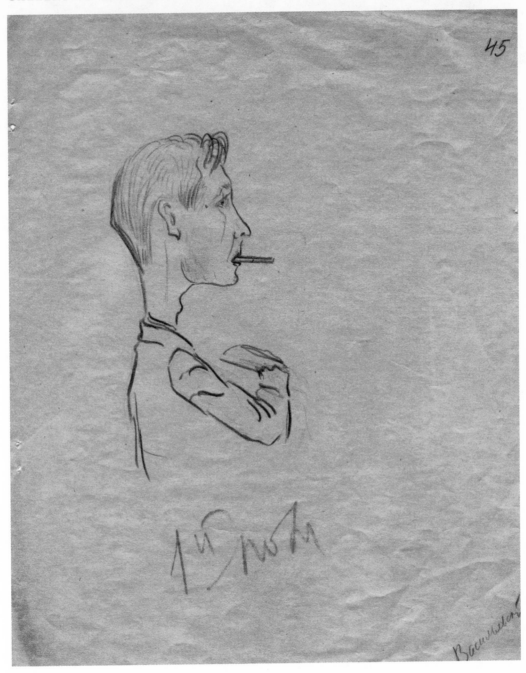

Fig. 86.
YE. M. YAROSLAVSKY, *V. N. Vasilievsky.* [1923.] Blue pencil. Inscription: "1st dep[uty]."
RGASPI, f. 74, op. 2, d. 168, l. 45.

Amayak Mararovich Nazaretian (1889–1937). A party member from 1905, he was head of the Bureau of the Secretariat of the Central Committee from 1922 to 1924. From 1924 to 1930 he headed the Trans-Caucasian territory party organization. He was arrested and executed in 1937.

Fig. 87.
Ye. M. Yaroslavsky, *A. M. Nazaretian*. [1923.] Pencil.
Inscriptions: "Provisional portrait, for lack of a better
one." "Chief."
RGASPI, f. 74, op. 2, d. 168, l. 44.

Yakov Arkadievich Yakovlev (born Epshtein, 1896–1938). A party member from 1913, he worked in the Central Committee apparatus from 1921 to 1924 and was people's commissar of agriculture from 1929 to 1934. He was arrested in 1937 and later shot.

Fig. 88.
Ye. M. Yaroslavsky, *Ya. A. Yakovlev.* [1923.] Blue pencil. Inscription: "Yakovlev 'Initiative.'"
RGASPI, f. 74, op. 2, d. 168, l. 38.

Demian Bedny (born Yefim Pridvorov, 1883–1945). A party member from 1912, he was a prominent Soviet poet.

Fig. 89.
Unknown artist, *D. Bedny*. Blue ink. Inscription: "This lyre sings
of Aleksei Rykov. Demian Bedny." Inscription by Rykov: "Looks
like D. B[edny] composed this."
RGASPI, f. 669, op. 1, d. 14, l. 156.

Nikolai Dmitrievich Kondratiev (1892–1938), a prominent Russian economist, specializing in agriculture. He was professor at the Moscow Agricultural Academy, and later became director of the Institute of Market of the People's Commissariat of Finances. He was arrested in 1930 and later executed.

Fig. 90.
UNKNOWN ARTIST, *N. D. Kondratiev.* Pencil. Inscription: "Professor Kondratiev before attacking Strumilin." (Stanislav Strumilin was a distinguished Russian economist, statistician, and economic historian.)
RGASPI, f. 669, op. 1, d. 14, l. 155.

David Borisovich Riazanov (1870–1938). A party member from 1917, he was director of the Marx-Engels Institute from 1921 to 1931. In 1929 he was elected a member of the Academy of Sciences. He was arrested in 1937 and later executed.

Fig. 91.
YE. M. YAROSLAVSKY, *D. B. Riazanov.* 24 January 1929.
Blue pencil. Inscription by the artist: "One of the new
Academy members."
RGASPI, f. 74, op. 2, d. 169, l. 80.

Otto Yulievich Shmidt (1891–1956), scientist and explorer responsible for the Soviet program of exploration of the Arctic. From 1921 to 1924 he was head of the State Publishing House, and from 1932 to 1939 head of the Northern Sea Ways Management.

Fig. 92.
V. I. Mezhlauk, *O. Yu. Shmidt.*
Pencil. Inscription by the artist:
"Oh! Greetings to an old
friend! We have decided to
award you the honorary walrus
title!" On the reverse: "VII
congress of Soviets.
Jan[uary] 1935."
RGASPI, f. 74, op. 2, d. 170, l. 41.

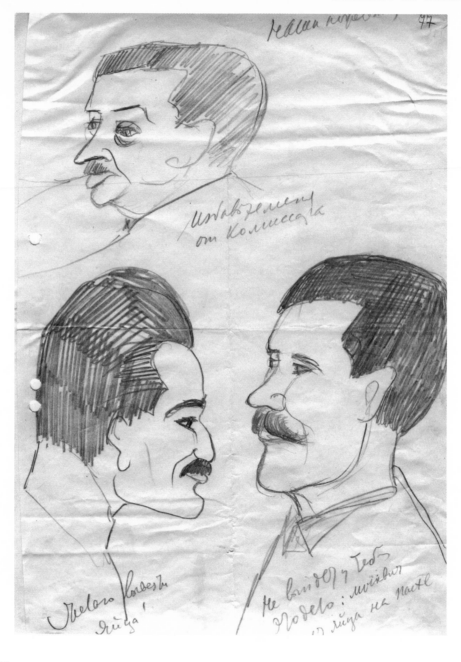

Fig. 93.
YE. M. YAROSLAVSKY, *M. P. Tomsky, A. I. Mikoyan, N. A. Uglanov.* [22 March 1928.] Pencil.
Inscriptions: "Our wishes." Tomsky: "Save me from the commissar." Mikoyan: "I want to
export eggs!" Uglanov: "You won't succeed: Muscovites will gobble up the eggs on Easter."
RGASPI, f. 74, op. 2, d. 169, l. 77.

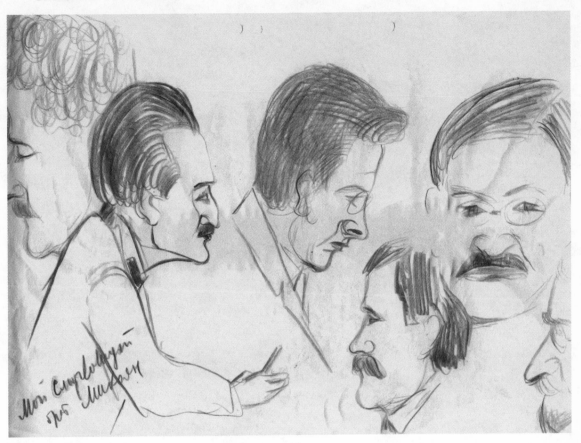

Fig. 94.
YE. M. YAROSLAVSKY, *G. K. Ordzhonikidze, A. I. Mikoyan,*
Ya. E. Rudzutak(?), N. A. Uglanov, V. M. Molotov, M. I. Kalinin.
Blue and red pencil. Inscription by the artist: "My dark-skinned
brother Mikoyan."
RGASPI, f. 74, op. 2, d. 169, l. 79.

PART 2

Comrades and Problems

Deviations and Oppositions

Struggles for leadership and personal conflicts between politicians are fertile grounds for caricaturists. The fight between Lenin's heirs for the right to determine the political course of the nation, disguised as the struggle for the Leninist "general line," attracted the close attention of the cartoonists. Political pluralism in the highest level of the Soviet party had its last hurrah in the late 1920s. Only some of the stormy conflicts of those years resulted from the clash of personal ambitions: at stake was the future of the huge country.

Most important, the future of the New Economic Policy (NEP) had to be decided. The NEP, introduced at the end of the Civil War to help galvanize the failing economy, allowed for the limited liberalization of markets and private enterprise. Debates attempting to determine whether the party should build on the NEP's success or scale it back caused the disintegration of the ruling triumvirate—Stalin, Zinoviev, and Kamenev—that had been forged in the struggle against Trotsky. In the fall of 1925, on the eve of the fourteenth congress of the VKP(b), the so-called Leningrad opposition, led by Zinoviev, raised the question of "right deviation" in the party, evoking the image of the kulaks (rich peasants) and the *nepmani*, urban entrepreneurs who profited from the New Economic Policy. Stalin, who controlled the party apparatus, managed to mobilize the majority of its members, including some prominent Old Bolsheviks. The oppositionists Zinoviev and Kamenev found themselves isolated, and were forced to recant. This scenario recurred during every future internal conflict in the party.

The first drawing in this section is not dated, but it is obvious when it was created.

After the defeat at the fourteenth congress, Zinoviev did not capitulate and was willing to reuse those perpetual bogeymen, the kulak and the nepman, in order to pressure the party leaders from the left (fig. 95). Everybody knew that yesterday's opposition-ists were preparing their revenge. The inscription on the drawing points to the coming plenum of the Central Committee. At that plenum, in July 1929, the "left" and "right" oppositions of Trotsky, Kamenev, and Zinoviev came together to form a "united oppo-sition" against Stalin. This brought the conflict in the party leadership to a climax.

Some plenum participants attempted to take the middle ground. Without support-ing the opposition, they issued their own draft resolution criticizing Stalin's violations of party democracy. The resolution noted: "It is only possible to overcome the existing disagreements through the active participation of the party's masses in a discussion of the questions important to the party. Every party member has to be able to take an active part in the life of the party without fearing persecution for nonconformity." The Stalinist majority rejected this proposition. Ivar Smilga, who was the first to sign the buffer resolution, became the subject of one of Bukharin's cartoons (fig. 98).

Smilga, who had been one of the leaders of the State Planning Committee, helped prepare the opposition's economic platform for the fifteenth party conference (26 Oc-tober–3 November 1926). The true leader, however, was Piatakov. Oppositionists urged accelerating industrial development and reversing the New Economic Policy re-forms. Ironically, many of these proposals would later be incorporated in the Stalin-ist policy of the "great turning point." Piatakov, in particular, stressed that "the main goal is to develop both a comprehensive plan for national economic development and a long-term plan of the development of industry, transportation, and electricity." The resulting "five-year industrial orientation" is almost indistinguishable from the future five-year plans.

At the conference, the chairman of the government, Rykov, representing the ma-jority in the Central Committee, gave a report on the state of the economy. He ac-knowledged the end of the rebuilding period (associated with the NEP) and the begin-ning of the socialist reconstruction (rapid advance to socialism), but opposed sharp shifts in policy. Even though the plan of the majority and the platform of the opposi-tion differed only in details, neither side was prepared to make concessions. The reason was not the difference in economic views. The economic discussion was only a smoke-screen for the struggle for leadership. Oppositionists looked like Lilliputians in the palm of Gulliver's hand (fig. 99).

Another caricature refers to "scissors," an economic term describing the difference between prices of industrial goods and prices of agricultural produce, which favored industry (fig. 100). In the theses written in September 1926 for the fifteenth party conference, Trotsky used this term to characterize the policy of his opponents: "There is a clear and growing discrepancy between the proclaimed course and the de facto policy toward industry, countryside, and the party—a kind of political scissors. . . . This political gap indicates the degree of capitulation. The same gap marks the level of Stalinist coercion: the farther the political practice is from the resolutions, i.e., the less it corresponds to the party's social composition and its traditions, the less it is possible to conduct this policy in a normal party manner, the greater is the role of personal appointments and repressions."

The cartoon appeared not earlier than August 1926, when Mikoyan, at Stalin's urging, replaced the oppositionist Kamenev as the people's commissar of foreign and domestic trade. Mikoyan and his deputy, Nikolai B. Eismont, were depicted as the owners of the "scissors wholesale and retail" company. Stalin could also have scribbled his comment in 1927 when the Politburo and the Central Control Commission (CCC) Presidium deliberated the fate of the oppositionists.

At first, the CCC Presidium, which greatly contributed to the badgering of the "united opposition," tried to prevent the discussion from becoming personal and non-political. N. I. Smirnov, editor-in-chief of the *Rabochaia gazeta,* was reprimanded for publishing lampoons insulting the oppositionists in the 9 November 1926 issue. The CCC Presidium stressed that "the cartoon depictions of the party members are inadmissible and harmful." However, as the internecine conflict grew, the stated ethical norms were more often and easily violated, especially within the narrow circle of party leaders. The artists' drawings are merciless and irreverent (fig. 97).

The only watercolor in the collection shows Lev Kamenev painting the "Lion" Trotsky into a tiger (fig. 96). Several other artists exploited this theme; one labeled his work "the major overhaul of Trotskyism." The cartoon refers to the debate between Trotsky and the majority of the Central Committee. In the course of the argument Trotsky mentioned the prime minister of France, Georges Clemenceau, who had been called "the French tiger" for establishing a military dictatorship in 1917. It did not take long for the party propaganda to accuse Trotsky of nurturing dictatorial plans. He tried in vain to justify himself by insisting that in politics "one cannot make a single step without drawing on the examples of the tactics of the alien classes."

The oppositionists, convinced of their intellectual superiority, used satire to get back at their opponents. One collage shows Stalin as a petty despot surrounded by hustling bootlickers (fig. 101). The pooch licking the master's boots is Bukharin. (Ten years later he would again be drawn as an animal; fig. 171.) The artist (possibly Radek) ridiculed Stalin's Caucasian accent: his speech in broken Russian is carefully constructed out of newspaper type.

Another caricature by the oppositionists portrays Stalin as an old-regime gendarme, trampling on the party's democratic principles and imprisoning the best Bolsheviks (fig. 102). This time, instead of Bukharin, it is Yaroslavsky prostrate at the master's feet. After their defeat at the fifteenth party congress, supporters of Trotsky and Zinoviev turned to the underground propaganda methods of the prerevolutionary period: this caricature was copied by hectograph, colored by hand, and distributed as a leaflet. The artist, who signed as "Ovod" (gadfly), clearly hit the mark with his depiction of the resurgence of authoritarianism in Russia.

Raging conflict between the feuding camps engrossed even the relatively peaceful Bukharin, who drew Sergo Ordzhonikidze preparing for a ritual immolation of the enemies (fig. 103). The date and inscription on the drawing imply a private meeting of the Stalin-Bukharin group during which plans were made to remove the opposition from party leadership. Apparently, the emotional Caucasian Sergo displayed a most ferocious attitude. The plenum that opened the next day passed a resolution about removing the oppositionists from the Central Committee, after which they recanted and expressed readiness for constructive dialogue. For the time being, they got off easy: Trotsky and Zinoviev received a "harsh reprimand and warning."

The fifteenth party congress (in December 1927) was no longer a platform for equal representation. The oppositionists who dared to speak were subjected to obstruction, hissed at, and literally chased off the podium. Drawings by M. L. Belotsky indicate the atmosphere of the congress, dominated by the victorious party apparatchiks. The transcript of the congress includes remarks from the audience addressed to Nikolai I. Muralov: "Nikolai Ivanovich, shame on you, drop the Trotsky crib sheet!" (fig. 106). Finally, Muralov lost his temper: "Comrades, if you are told that you have killed your wife, eaten up your grandfather, ripped off the head of your grandmother—how are you going to feel, how are you going to disprove it?" Despite his attempts to pacify the two sides, S. K. Minin, a delegate from Leningrad, had to leave the podium due to obstruction (fig. 105).

The image of the all-party gendarme is used again (more sympathetically this time) by Krzhizhanovsky, who portrayed Stalin as an executioner (fig. 104). Stalin is still merely "conducting the will of the party," as he prepares to whip the oppositionists, who readily lower their pants. Later this image would acquire a different, darker meaning, and many of the party members who had stood behind Stalin fell victim to his whip.

Less than a year after the defeat of the united opposition, Stalin singled out new victims: his former loyal supporters Bukharin, Rykov, and Tomsky were accused of right deviation. This time Bukharin, who used to promote free speech, became an object of political satire. One of the conditions for the right oppositionists to return to the collective work in the Politburo, agreed to in November 1928, was the punishment of the author of a caricature ridiculing Bukharin's becoming a member of the Academy of Sciences. The caricature appeared in the Leningrad magazine *Pushka*. An angry Bukharin demanded that the author be "arrested if he is not a party member or be tried by the party if he is a party member." A few months later Ordzhonikidze reported to the Central Committee plenum: "The magazine is closed, the editor fired, and the artist arrested."

As with the united opposition, attempts to establish constructive collaboration with the right opposition turned out to be no more than Stalin's complicated game. In the spring of 1929, Bukharin's supporters were isolated or had switched sides, and the party apparatus was preparing for the final assault on him. At that time cartoons appeared scoffing at the panic-mongering by the "rightists" (figs. 107, 108). Stalin once said that "the Bukharin group lives in the past . . . and does not understand the necessity of the new forms of struggle. As a result, they are blind, confused, and panicked in the face of difficulties." The artist used this perception in combination with the scary image of a giant cockroach from a well-known tale by Kornei Chukovsky. Noticing the roach's antennae, a frightened Rykov crosses himself, and a shaken Bukharin displays yet another political statement about the wrong policy of the Central Committee. The artist is ridiculing Bukharin's inclination toward theorizing as well as his unusual hobby: collecting rare insects.

The only representative of the right deviation who retained his post after its defeat was Rykov. He was subjected to measured badgering. Stalin said that "the Chairman of the Council of People's Commissars has to put into practice the party resolutions on a daily basis, and to take part in preparing them. Is this being done? No, unfortunately. That is the reason for our dissatisfaction." Rykov felt growing pressure not only from the Politburo members but from his own subordinates, who knew perfectly well that their boss was hanging by a thread. At the 25 April 1930 Politburo session Rykov maintained a stiff silence, further irritating his adversaries (fig. 109).

In December 1930, Molotov, a loyal Stalinist, replaced Rykov as the head of government. Rykov was demoted to the position of people's commissar of communications. Around this time, Mezhlauk produced an inoffensive caricature of Rykov clamoring for a campaign against slovenliness in the postal sector (fig. 110). At the February–March 1937 plenum of the Central Committee, a former worker from Rykov's secretariat quoted the dismayed leader's reaction to his demotion: "So much for the Politburo, so much for the cooperation: here I am, a postmaster." Whether or not he really said it, when the time came, the architects of the Great Terror used these words to accuse Rykov of plotting to create terrorist groups. Thus a poisonous mixture of truth and lies assisted Stalin in the liquidation of his former comrades. They were accused first of various deviations, then of wrecking, and finally, of terror and espionage.

Fig. 95.
V. I. Mezhlauk, *G. Ye. Zinoviev.* Black and red pencil. Inscription by the artist: "Masha, tonight is the plenum of the Central Committee. Please clean the kulak and the nepman, and, after I return, sprinkle them with mothballs: we won't need them until fall." On the box: "Leningrad, December 1925." On the reverse: "To Zinoviev."

RGASPI, f. 74, op. 2, d. 168, l. 21.

Fig. 96.
V. I. MEZHLAUK, *L. D. Trotsky*
and L. B. Kamenev. Watercolor.
RGASPI, f. 74, op. 2, d. 169, l. 99.

Fig. 97.
V. I. MEZHLAUK, *L. B. Kamenev, L. D. Trotsky, G. Ye. Zinoviev.* Pencil. Inscription by the artist:
"The yard-keeper, the leader, and the rear-guard* of the opposition bloc according to Stalin-Uglanov.
[Footnote at bottom:] *Alias member of the society to support old fathers." (In early October 1926,
Zinoviev went to Leningrad to attend the workers' meetings to promote the platform of the opposition.
As a result, he missed a Politburo session. According to a document in the archive [f. 17, op. 2, d. 294,
l. 18], when asked Zinoviev's whereabouts, "Comrade Kamenev responded that his dad had gotten
sick, and he went to see his dad.")

RGASPI, f. 669, op. 1, d. 14, l. 186.

Fig. 98.
N. I. Bukharin, *I. T. Smilga*. Pencil. Inscription by the artist:
"A cartoon of the 'buffer.'" Inscription at the top by Stalin:
"To all members of the Plenum."
RGASPI, f. 326, op. 2, d. 19, l. 21.

Fig. 99.
V. I. Mezhlauk, *A. I. Rykov, G. L. Piatakov, L. B. Kamenev, I. T. Smilga.* Pencil. Inscription by the artist: "A. I. Rykov prepares for the report at the 15th party conference (analysis of the 'economic platform' of the opposition—Piatakov, Kamenev, Smilga)." Rykov: "They all wear glasses, but one cannot see them without glasses."

RGASPI, f. 669, op. 1, d. 14, l. 183.

Fig. 100.

V. I. Mezhlauk, *A. I. Mikoyan, I. T. Smilga, L. D. Trotsky.* Pencil. Inscription by the artist: "Mikoyan: 'Which [scissors] would you like?' Tr[otsky]: 'I prefer the ones without moral wear.' Sm[ilga]: 'I want seasonal: with a heavier peasant's end.'" Text of the ad: "Wholesale and retail, scissors industrial-agricultural, private-cooperative, state retail-cooperative, etc. From best companies: State Planning Committee, Institute of Competition, People's Commissariat of Finances, People's Commissariat of Trade, Central Statistical Board, and others. A. I. Mikoyan, N. B. Eismont and Co." Inscription at the top by Stalin: "To all members of the Politburo and Presidium of the C[entral] C[ontrol] C[ommission]."

RGASPI, f. 74, op. 2, d. 170, l. 136.

Fig. 101.
K. RADEK, *After discussion. I. V. Stalin, Ya. E. Rudzutak, N. I. Bukharin.* Collage.
RGASPI, f. 326, op. 2, d. 19, l. 7.

Fig. 102.
UNKNOWN ARTIST, *I. V. Stalin and Ye. M. Yaroslavsky.* 1927. Colored pencils. Inscription by the artist: "All-party oppressor and gendarme Stalin . . . and his sleuth-dog Yaroslavka." The prison cell at right is labeled "party apparatus," and the prisoner behind bars is labeled "VKP," the initials of the Communist Party. Stalin is trampling on "party democracy" and has stuck the "Resolutions of the 15th congress" in his bootleg.

RGASPI, f. 74, op. 2, d. 168, l. 184.

Fig. 103.
N. I. Bukharin, *G. K. Ordzhonikidze.* Pencil. Inscription by the artist: "Saint Sergoshvili before the immolation of his victims." Inscription by Voroshilov: "Private meeting before the plenum of the Central Committee and the Central Control Commission. 28 July [19]27. Drawn by Bukhashka."
RGASPI, f. 74, op. 2, d. 168, l. 135.

Fig. 104.
G. M. Krzhizhanovsky(?), *I. T. Smilga, G. Ye. Zinoviev, L. B. Kamenev, L. D. Trotsky, and I. V. Stalin.* Green ink. Inscription by the artist: "Top secret. Bulletin on the opposition disease." Inscription: "Drawn by Kryzhanovsky."
RGASPI, f. 668, op. 1, d. 14, l. 172.

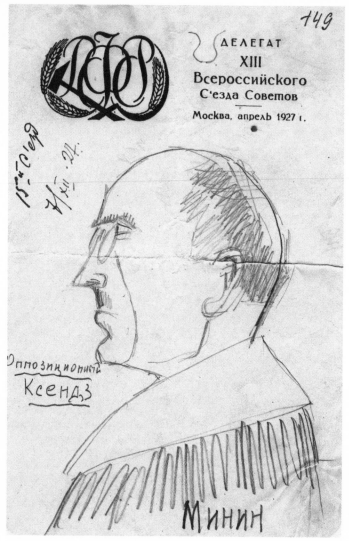

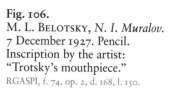

Fig. 105.
M. L. Belotsky, *S. K. Minin.*
7 December 1927. Pencil.
Inscription by the artist:
"Opposition ksendz [from
ksiądz, Polish for Catholic
priest] Minin." On the reverse:
"To C. Voroshilov from
Belotsky."
RGASPI, f. 74, op. 2, d. 168, l. 149–149 rev.

Fig. 106.
M. L. Belotsky, *N. I. Muralov.*
7 December 1927. Pencil.
Inscription by the artist:
"Trotsky's mouthpiece."
RGASPI, f. 74, op. 2, d. 168, l. 150.

Fig. 107.
V. I. Mezhlauk, *A. I. Rykov, N. I. Bukharin, M. P. Tomsky.* [1929.] Violet ink. Inscriptions by the artist: Rykov (at left): "Heaven help us!! A catastrophe!!! End of Soviet Power!!" Bukharin (center): "The policy of the Central Committee has brought the country to ruin!!!" Tomsky (right): "You never know what might happen."
RGASPI, f. 74, op. 2, d. 169, l. 97.

Fig. 108.
V. I. Mezhlauk, *A. I. Rykov, N. I. Bukharin, M. P. Tomsky.* [1929.] Violet ink. Inscription by the artist: "Rykov: 'Hum, a cockroach . . . Pah! What a muck! I'm not a bit scared!' Bukharin: 'Sure, it is a cockroach, ha-ha-ha! I knew it, I even brought a tool for this *insectum!* It's but an ordinary *ortopterus, blata orientalis,* or, in other words, *cockroachius!*' Tomsky: 'Oh well. Still, let's wait until spring—you never know what might happen!'"
RGASPI, f. 74, op. 2, d. 169, l. 98.

Fig. 109.
V. I. MEZHLAUK, *A. I. Rykov.*
25 April 1930. Black ink.
Inscription by the artist: " 'Is
it true that Rykov stopped
stuttering?' — 'That's right,
because they don't let him utter
a word.' (From the right-leaning
sources)."

RGASPI, f. 74, op. 2, d. 169, l. 90.

Fig. 110.
V. I. MEZHLAUK, *A. I. Rykov.* [1930.] Pencil. Inscription by the
artist: "A. I. Rykov rushes to attack."

RGASPI, f. 74, op. 2, d. 170, l. 17.

Supplementary Agendas

After the stormy period of the late 1920s–early 1930s, the ruling party overcame internal oppositions and proclaimed the "advance of socialism on all fronts." Virtually no aspect of public life, the economy, or culture remained unchanged. The Stalinist revolution of the 1930s is well researched and documented. Much less is known, however, about how these processes affected the style of work and personal relations in the ruling elite. The revolutionary camaraderie and tradition of collective leadership slowly succumbed to suffocating ideological intolerance and personal dictatorship. Together with the recently published correspondence of the Politburo members, drawings in this section help reveal the secret mechanisms of the Soviet political machine of that period.

During the 15 March 1931 session of the Politburo, Valery Mezhlauk made a series of drawings. Combined with available documents, these images show how frequently the discussions went beyond the formal agenda. They serve as a quasi-transcript of the session, revealing the real tension and emotions behind the discussion. Only the report by Krzhizhanovsky on the electrification of the main industrial regions was on the agenda. Neither Kalinin nor Voroshilov, also pictured by Mezhlauk, gave planned speeches. His drawings are probably a reaction to their pugnacious remarks during the debate.

One of the first problems discussed on 15 March was the delivery of Donetsk coal to Moscow and Leningrad. Shortages of coal resulted from inadequate transport service, but the Politburo members suspected that the leaders of the coal-mining regions, holding on to the valuable resource, were at fault. It seems that Kalinin lashed out at the Ukrainian leader, noting that it might be spring and warm weather in the Ukraine, but in Moscow people were freezing (fig. 112).

Correspondence between Stalin and Voroshilov shows that the latter constantly complained about the attempts to cut the military budget. Another such attempt at the meeting made the people's commissar of defense jump and curse (fig. 111). An emotional Ordzhonikidze is shown being even less courteous when reprimanding N. I. Pakhomov of Nizhny Novgorod for being late (fig. 114).

Foreign policy issues discussed by the Politburo were usually top secret. The protocols were kept in special files. As a result, there are virtually no drawings associated with these discussions. One of the few exceptions is the caricature of Uncle Sam in connection with the attempts by the Soviet government to obtain large amounts of credit (fig. 118). The drawing of Litvinov, people's commissar of foreign affairs, at a lavishly laid table appeared on the eve of his foreign tour. The artist depicted the details of the alien bourgeois world, which looks very much like a nepman restaurant, including monocle, palm tree, caviar, and champagne (fig. 115). Another picture of Litvinov, portraying him as a ballerina, hints at both his nimbleness as a diplomat and his frequent trips abroad (fig. 116). Mezhlauk also smiles at the preparations for Iosif Kosior's visit to the United States, with sad Russian ladies sending him off, and an African-American woman welcoming him (fig. 117).

In the early 1930s, Andrei Bubnov was assigned to save the failing education system, which party documents called the weak link of the socialist construction. Judging from the drawing, Bubnov was not quite confident in the success of this endeavor (fig. 121). The "cocky" portrait of the vice president of the Soviet Academy of Sciences is even less optimistic in terms of the future of Soviet science (fig. 120).

After Bukharin left *Pravda* in 1929, so did many of his supporters. One of the caricatures shows M. A. Saveliev and N. N. Popov, members of the editorial board, dancing to the tune of Lev Z. Mekhlis, the editor-in-chief (only his hat is visible; fig. 124). Two other caricatures picked on the stellar career of Mekhlis and the atmosphere of crackdown in Soviet society (figs. 125, 126). In June 1932–March 1933, the newspaper of the People's Commissariat of Heavy Industry, *Za industrializatsiu,* was publishing a discussion of the economic reform. The newspaper advocated moving away from vertical structures and centralized supplies in industry, and favored economic self-sufficiency for the enterprises and their reliance on the market to sell manufactured products. On 19 and 24 March, *Pravda* thundered with two editorials, which branded the discussion as a defeatist deviation from the party general line. Obviously, Mekhlis had coordinated this attack with Stalin, because it was aimed at Ordzhonikidze, the powerful people's commissar of heavy industry. On 4 April 1933, the Politburo approved *Pravda*'s position. The editor of *Za industrializatsiu,* V. S. Bogushevsky, was fired, and the newspaper staff was purged. I. I. Dolnikov, who initiated the discussion, was relieved of his post in the Central Committee apparatus and sent off to the provinces.

Several pictures serve as illustrations of the gradual empowerment of Stalin in the early 1930s. The secretary general enjoyed extemporaneously asking questions that were not on the Politburo agenda, often in order to humiliate his comrades. It was his way of showing who was really the master of the house. The most criticized area was transportation, but leaders of other industries were not immune from Stalin's sudden angry and sarcastic outbursts. On 5 March 1934, Stalin arrived at the Politburo meeting in bad temper. He began by blasting the railroad crashes and demanding public trials for those responsible. Next he accused the Goznak (the state mint) of printing money on bad paper. Apparently he was not happy with the way the new banknotes looked.

On 20 March 1934, the special commission reported on the results of its investigation of the banknote issue. Mezhlauk portrayed the head of Goznak, T. T. Yenukidze, throwing rolls of money at his opponents (fig. 123). Apparently, the leaders accused of negligence did not simply repent, but rather attempted to counterattack. We will never know what arguments they used, but they were hardly helpful. Stalin personally drafted the resolution about poor-quality bills, and it was approved without change. The final line reads like a conviction: "Consider it proved that comrades Grinko and Kalamanovich manifested negligence in this issue." M. I. Kalamanovich was soon removed from his job as chairman of the board of the State Bank. Grigory Grinko managed to hold on to his post as the people's commissar of finances—until his arrest.

Another set of drawings deals with the negative phenomena (drunkenness, bureaucratism, philistinism) that the Soviet propaganda tirelessly attacked for many years. These caricatures resemble those published in the official press. Very interesting is Mezhlauk's portrayal of "philistines" who voice their opinion (fig. 129). He is clearly opposed to their quite understandable expectation that feeding the country should come before building the glorious future. Naturally, when this future seems to be so close, small things like the lack of necessities become secondary. It was the way most Stalinist bureaucrats were genuinely thinking. With the rare exception of such visible cases as fatal train accidents (figs. 153–156), the Bolshevik elite showed little sympathy for the plight of ordinary people.

They did have plenty of sympathy for themselves, as they suffered through long meetings and waited for a session to start. They relieved boredom by walking around, playing chess, and chatting (fig. 132). This, however, is an image from the relatively liberal 1920s. In the 1930s they were all standing at attention, and only the bravest dared to eavesdrop at the door (fig. 134). While these are not actual photographs, these pictures are in their own way snapshots of the spirit in the sanctum sanctorum of the Bolshevik Olympus.

The facial expressions of speakers and audiences can be quite telling. On 8 March

1933, the Politburo discussed the situation in coal mining (fig. 131). The drawing shows Iosif Kosior of the People's Commissariat of Heavy Industry vigorously attacking the flaws of Donetsk miners. The head of the Ukrainian party organization, Ivan A. Akulov, looks as though he has been sentenced to death. Kuibyshev, chairman of the State Planning Committee, also feels the heat and considers his line of defense.

A prominent contemporary caricaturist, M. Zlatkovsky, noted the "unpolished style" of the Soviet caricatures of the 1930s, "suitable for people of low cultural and esthetical level." This fully applies to the drawings of the leaders, some of which are strikingly primitive. Still, it is important to keep in mind that these drawings were made for internal use by a narrow circle of comrades and were certainly not intended for publication seventy-five years later.

It is easy to understand the boredom that resulted from attending the annoying gala sessions of the rubber-stamp Soviet parliament. One cartoon shows Mikhail Kalinin at the eighth congress of Soviets (November–December 1936), frustrated by the endless talk of the Urals representative, I. D. Kabakov. So the "all-union elder" dispatches Semyon Budionny on a reconnaissance mission to see whether the speaker remembers about the time limit (fig. 133). Another picture lampoons the Georgian deputy, T. F. Makharadze, for having problems finishing his long speech (fig. 136). Such low blows and crude humor were customary among Stalinist cadres. Another drawing by Mezhlauk, who usually catered to the tastes and preferences of the leaders, depicts their favorite scapegoat, Briukhanov (fig. 135). This cartoon was created during a Politburo discussion of the state budget. Such sessions consistently turned out to be torturous for the people's commissar of finances. This drawing was mistakenly attributed to Stalin in earlier publications. Stalin only wrote his simple comment, evoking the medieval witch trials in which a tied-up woman was thrown into a river. If she did not sink, she was considered a witch. By addressing his comment to all Politburo members, Stalin made sure that they imagined themselves in poor Briukhanov's place.

The final set of drawings is a friendly duel between the two leading caricaturists — Mezhlauk and Bukharin. Mezhlauk did not like the portrait of him that was published in *Izvestia* on 8 February 1935. Since Bukharin was the editor-in-chief of that newspaper, he became the object of Mezhlauk's wrath (fig. 137). Bukharin responded by shaming his opponent in his own way (fig. 138). This exchange took place at the session of the Labor and Defense Council on 10 February 1935 and was probably continued after that.

In contrast with the caricatures from the turbulent 1920s, drawings in this section of the album have one thing in common: there is no enemy in them. The artists are indulgent toward their subjects, at worst portraying them as confused or simple-minded blunderers. They were all part of the family of the rising nomenklatura, with its caste identity and common interests. Even the portrait of a fat-bottomed bureaucrat with a "tea-belly" is more comical than disgusting.

The artists clearly shared the hopes and fears of their subjects—speakers patiently awaiting their turn, economists held responsible for the blunders of forced industrialization, diplomats compelled to strike a balance between traditional etiquette and the requirements imposed by the revolutionary moral code. This sense of solidarity among the Soviet elite of the 1930s increasingly irritated Stalin and became one of the catalysts of the mass purges.

Fig. 111.
V. I. Mezhlauk, *K. Ye. Voroshilov.* 15 March 1931. Pencil. Inscription by the artist: "What!!!??
My budget?! Yevtrigom, evtrugom, the Blessed Virgin!!!" (The words and the meaning of the
cursing are unclear.)

RGASPI, f. 74, op. 2, d. 169, l. 124.

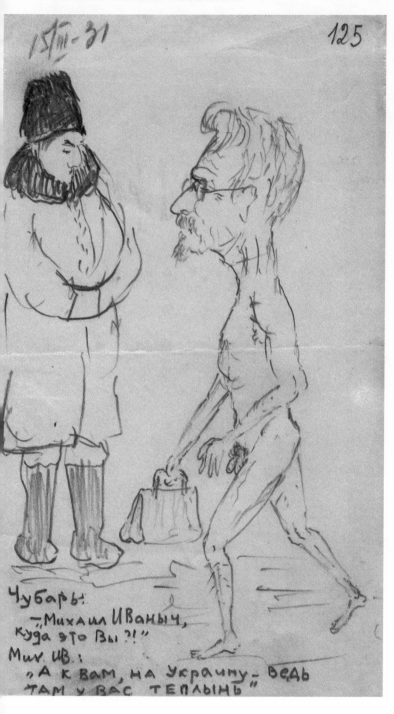

Fig. 112.
V. I. MEZHLAUK, *M. I. Kalinin,
V. Ya. Chubar*. 15 March 1931.
Pencil. Inscription by the artist:
"Chubar: 'Mikhail Ivanovich
[Kalinin], where are you going?'
Mikh[ail] Iv[anovich]: 'To that
Ukraine of yours—they say it's
really warm there.'" On the
reverse: "To K[liment]
Yefr[emovich Voroshilov]."
RGASPI, f. 74, op. 2, d. 169, l. 125–125 rev.

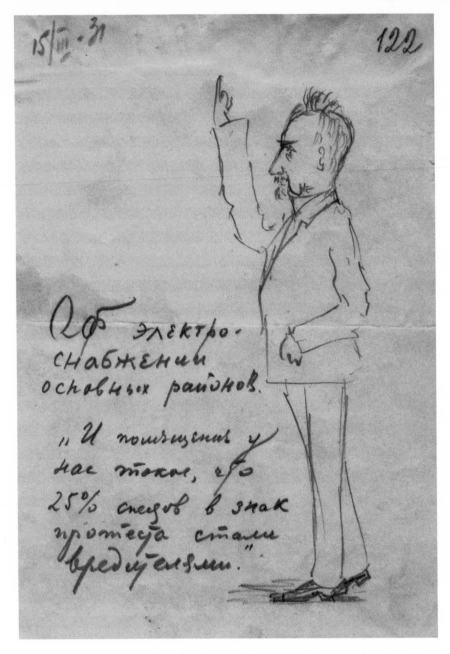

Fig. 113.
V. I. Mezhlauk, *G. M. Krzhizhanovsky.* 15 March 1931. Pencil. Inscription by the artist: "On the electrification of the main regions. 'The situation is such that 25 percent of all specialists became wreckers in protest.'"
RGASPI, f. 74, op. 2, d. 169, l. 122.

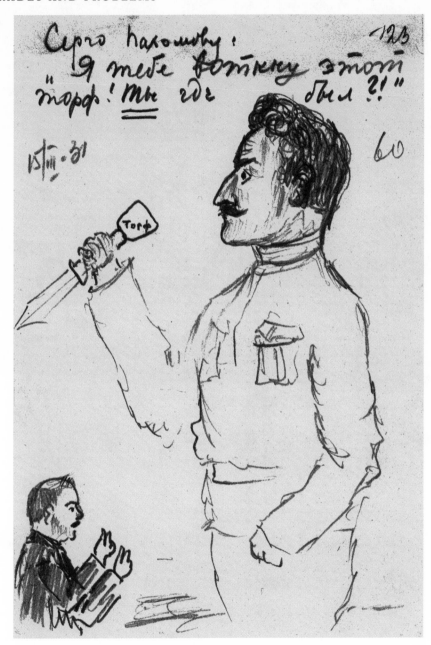

Fig. 114.
V. I. MEZHLAUK, *G. K. Ordzhonikidze and N. I. Pakhomov.* 15 March 1931. Pencil. Inscription by the artist: "Sergo [Ordzhonikidze] to Pakhomov: 'I'm gonna stick this "peat" in you! Where have *you* been?!'"

RGASPI, f. 74, op. 2, d. 169, l. 123.

Fig. 115.
UNKNOWN ARTIST, *M. M. Litvinov.* 25 April 1930. Red ink. Inscription by the artist: "M. M. Litvinov: 'From time to time I am compelled to make this great sacrifice.'"
RGASPI, f. 74, op. 2, d. 169, l. 87.

Fig. 116.
V. I. MEZHLAUK, *M. M. Litvinov.* Black ink. Inscription: "La donna e mobile" ("The lady is fickle," an aria from *Rigoletto*).
RGASPI, f. 669, op. 1, d. 14, l. 150.

Fig. 117.
V. I. MEZHLAUK, *I. V. Kosior*. Black, red, and blue pencil. Inscription by the artist: "Iosenka, for whom are you forsaking us? USSR. Iosenka, welcome! USA."
RGASPI, f. 74, op. 2, d. 169, l. 133.

Fig. 118.
UNKNOWN ARTIST, *A. I. Rykov.*
Black ink. Inscription by the
artist: "A[leksei] Iv[anovich
Rykov]: 'If we are going to
swindle them at all, we should
go all out!'"
RGASPI, f. 74, op. 2, d. 170, l. 113.

Fig. 119.
UNKNOWN ARTIST, *A. S.
Bubnov.* Blue ink. Inscription by
the artist: "A. S. Bubnov: 'Call
in my board! The session is
starting!'"
RGASPI, f. 74, op. 2, d. 170, l. 112.

Fig. 120.
UNKNOWN ARTIST, *G. M. Krzhizhanovsky.* Violet ink. Inscription by the artist: "Cock-a-doodle-doo!
Collective science! Glorious prospects! Cock-a-doodle-doo!!"
RGASPI, f. 74, op. 2, d. 170, l. 70.

Fig. 121.
V. I. Mezhlauk, *A. S. Bubnov.* Colored pencils. Inscription by the artist: "A horrible accident at the 4 January meeting: People's commissar of education Bubnov, distracted, grabbed a beet-root instead of the right link, and failed to pull education out." On the reverse: "To K. Ye. Voroshilov."
RGASPI, f. 74, op. 2, d. 170, l. 48.

Fig. 122.
Unknown artist, *A. S. Bubnov.* Pencil. Inscription: " 'Be it resolved, to secure the good of the commonweal, stable textbooks shall be rewritten.' Inscribed on the original in his own hand: Bubnov, Andrei." In the lower right corner, inscription by Stalin: "Additionally." (The education reform of the early 1930s included the unification of textbooks, which were called stable textbooks.)
RGASPI, f. 74, op. 2, d. 170, l. 49.

Fig. 123.
V. I. Mezhlauk, *T. T.*
Yenukidze. 20 March 1934.
Pencil. Inscription by the artist:
"C[omrade] Yenukidze rushed
to the offensive. 'Criticizing my
critics.'"
RGASPI, f. 74, op. 2, d. 170, l. 8.

Fig. 124.
V. I. Mezhlauk, *L. Z. Mekhlis,*
N. N. Popov, M. A. Saveliev.
20 June 1931. Pencil. Inscription
by the artist: "Disposition:
Saveliev: Popov: Mekhlis." On
the reverse, inscription by
Mezhlauk: "To K. Ye.
Voroshilov."
RGASPI, f. 74, op. 2, d. 169, l. 127.

Fig. 125.
V. I. MEZHLAUK, *V. S. Bogushevsky, L. Z. Mekhlis.* 4 April 1933. "Mekhlis to Bogushevsky: 'Wait patiently until I finish eating you.'"
RGASPI, f. 74, op. 2, d. 169, l. 163.

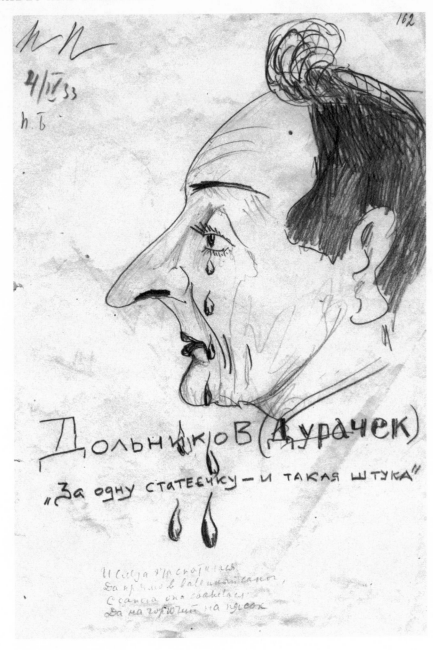

Fig. 126.
V. I. Mezhlauk, *I. I. Dolnikov.* 4 April 1933. Pencil. Inscription by the artist: "Dolnikov (little fool). 'For one small article—that's a nice thing.'" Inscription: "And the tear rolled / Right into a felt boot / From the boot it fell / Right on the hot sand."

RGASPI, f. 74, op. 2, d. 169, l. 162.

Fig. 127.
V. I. MEZHLAUK, *Evolutionary theory.* Blue pencil. Inscription by
the artist: "Evolutionary theory: a horse feeding on a palm tree
turns into a giraffe; a windbag economist who spends much time
at meetings turns into what is pictured." On the reverse:
"To K. Ye. Voroshilov."

RGASPI, f. 74, op. 2, d. 169, l. 152–152 rev.

Fig. 128.
V. I. MEZHLAUK, *"Death to
vodka!!!—one of these days."*
Black ink.

RGASPI, f. 74, op. 2, d. 169, l. 68.

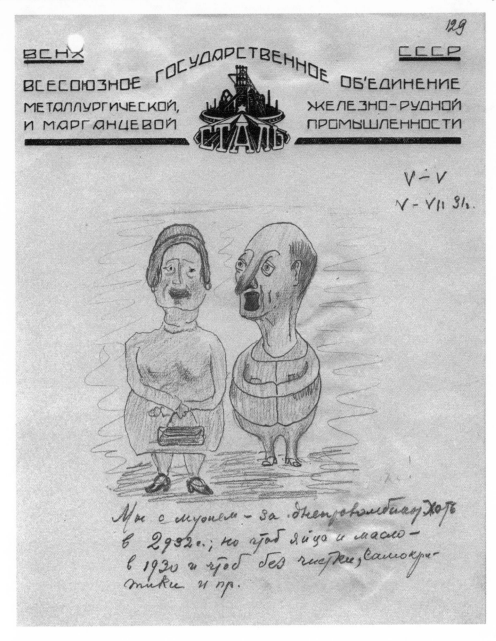

Fig. 129.
V. I. Mezhlauk, *"We have to have eggs and butter."* May–July 1931. Black, blue, and red pencil.
Inscription by the artist: "My husband and I are for the Dneprokhimkombinat [Dnepropetrovsk
Chemical Industrial Complex], even in the year 2932; but have to have eggs and butter in 1930,
and without purges, self-criticism, etc."
RGASPI, f. 74, op. 2, d. 169, l. 129.

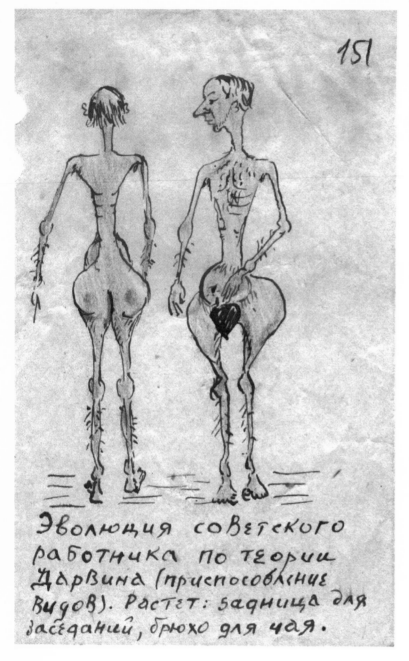

Эволюция советского
работника по теории
Дарвина (приспособление
видов). Растет: задница для
заседаний, брюхо для чая.

Fig. 130.
V. I. Mezhlauk, *Evolution of Soviet bureaucrat*. Violet ink, red pencil. Inscription by the artist: "Evolution of Soviet bureaucrat according to Darwin (adaptation of species). Enlarged bottom for [sitting at the] meetings, and belly for tea."
RGASPI, f. 74, op. 2, d. 169, l. 151.

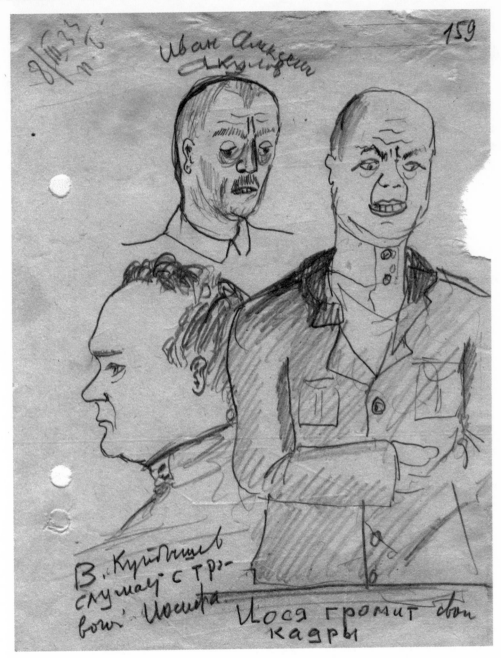

Fig. 131.
V. I. Mezhlauk, *V. V. Kuibyshev, I. A. Akulov, I. V. Kosior*. 8 March 1933. Pencil. Inscription: "Anxious V. Kuibyshev listens to Iosif [Kosior]. Iosia is blasting his cadres."

RGASPI, f. 74, op. 2, d. 169, l. 159.

Fig. 132.
V. I. MEZHLAUK, *What is happening in the speakers' room?* Blue and red pencil. Inscription on the reverse by the artist: "What is happening in the speakers' room when it is [already] 16:25, and the discussion has not gotten past the second issue on the agenda? Only the goalkeeper, C[omrade] Gordeyeva, is at her post."
RGASPI, f. 669, op. 1, d. 14, l. 178.

Fig. 133.
V. I. MEZHLAUK, *I. D. Kabakov, S. M. Budionny, M. I. Kalinin.* [November–December 1936.] Pencil. Inscription: "How Budionny went on a reconnaissance mission: when will the speaker finish."
RGASPI, f. 74, op. 2, d. 170, l. 67.

Fig. 134.
V. I. Mezhlauk, *"Well, let's open the Politburo session!"*
25 October 1930. Pencil.
RGASPI, f. 74, op. 2, d. 169, l. 108.

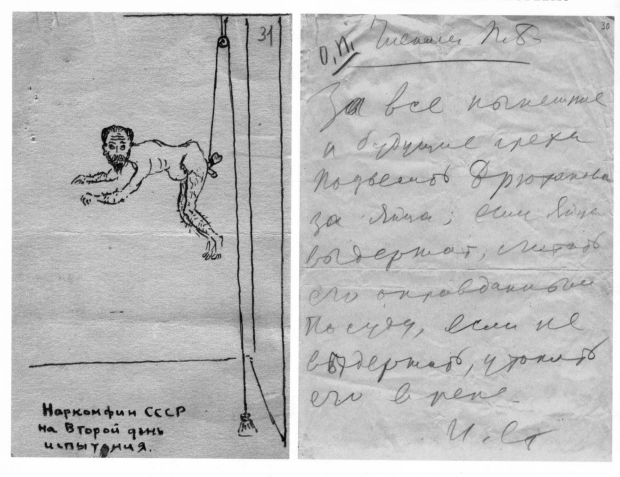

Fig. 135.
V. I. MEZHLAUK, N. P. Briukhanov. 5 April 1930. Black ink.
Inscription by the artist: "People's Commissar of Finances of the
USSR at the second day of trial." Note by Stalin, attached: "*To the
members of the P[olit]B[uro].* For all the sins, past and present, hang
Briukhanov by the balls. If the balls hold out, consider him
acquitted by trial. If they do not hold, drown him
in the river. I[osif] St[alin]."
RGASPI, f. 558, op. 11, d. 27, l. 31.

Fig. 136.
V. I. Mezhlauk, *T. F. Makharadze.* Pencil. Inscription by the artist: "T. F. Makharadze having trouble finishing." Inscription by Voroshilov: "Seventh congress, January 1935."
RGASPI, f. 74, op. 2, d. 170, l. 38.

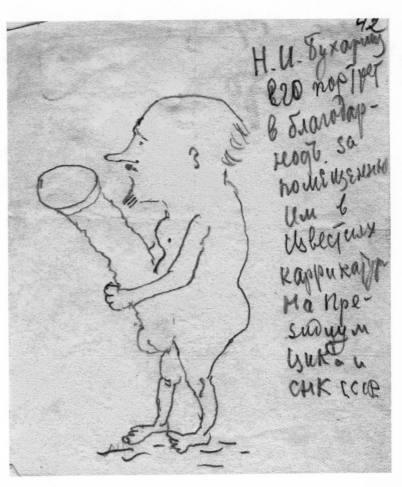

Fig. 137.
V. I. Mezhlauk, *N. I. Bukharin.* 10 March 1935. Pencil. Inscription by the artist: "To N. I. Bukharin, his portrait, in gratitude for posting in *Izvestia* caricatures on the CEC [Central Executive Committee] Presidium and the SNK [Council of People's Commissars] of the USSR."
RGASPI, f. 74, op. 2, d. 170, l. 42.

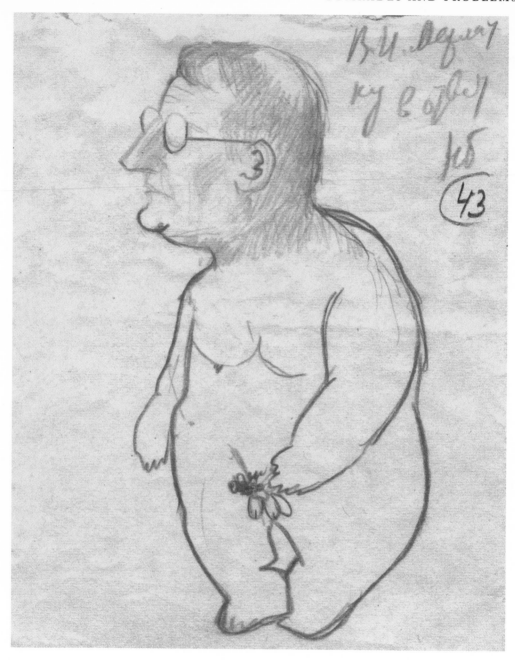

Fig. 138.
N. I. BUKHARIN, *V. I. Mezhlauk*. 10 March 1935. Red pencil. Inscription by the artist:
"To V. I. Mezhlauk in return. N[ikolai] B[ukharin]."
RGASPI, f. 74, op. 2, d. 170, l. 43.

Economic Conflicts and Rapid Industrialization

The majority of the drawings in the archival collection are related to economic problems. One of the most productive artists, Valery Mezhlauk, occupied high positions in economic management, and socialist industrialization of the country was a dominant theme in the 1930s. The ruling party literally dragged the country into a new era, crushing a centuries-old patriarchal way of life, breaking traditions, moving millions of people. Even those who were skeptical about the ability to achieve the goal of universal equality and prosperity and those who were victimized by the new regime had to admit the radical changes in the economy. New railroads, factories, and electric power stations rose in huge construction projects. As the USSR engaged in rapid industrial development, the rest of the world sank into depression. This was a powerful source of national pride.

The five-year plan goals were absolute imperatives for Stalinist cadres, and the drawings reveal their thinking and the methods used to achieve those goals. One can sense the administrative pressure from above and discern a complex web of institutional and interpersonal relations, a daily struggle of the captains of socialist industry for resources and capital investments.

This section opens with caricatures related to budget and finances. The demands of heavy industry made the problem of additional investment an oversized issue (fig. 141). Favoring industry resulted in inflation, scarcity of consumer goods, and wasted natural resources. But even the commissar of heavy industry, Ordzhonikidze, often failed to get what he needed without adequate political support (fig. 140).

Of all the struggles in the Kremlin, the battles fought over the flow of money were the most brutal. Suffice to remember the portraits of Soviet bankers in the first part of the book, or Stalin's commentary about the fate of Briukhanov. Similarly brutal is the representation of Piatakov, having ravaged his opponents in the fight for the heavy industry budget (fig. 142). Another telling image is a portrait of Mezhlauk, being strangled by a blast furnace come alive (fig. 144).

This album contains only a small sample of the drawings related to the economy. Most of them address very specific issues that never appear in the official documents. Deciphering the meaning of these images is as fascinating as reading fragmented ancient sources, and it is possible only through comprehensive analysis of their historical context. Thus, an inscription on the caricature depicting the deputy people's commissar of heavy industry Kaganovich (fig. 150) helps explain the inscription on the drawing of "failed equilibrists" (fig. 145), and even helps ascertain that Kaganovich is in that picture as well. On 20 February 1934, the Politburo reviewed the question of production of tractor plows for the spring sowing campaign. The protocol of the session contains harsh instructions to the departments in charge of the production of plows. Stalin amended the resolution by inscribing "personal responsibility of C[omrade] M. Kaganovich." This probably was in response to the latter's failed attempts to shift responsibility for failures to middlemen and suppliers.

The Marxist concept of overcoming conflicts after the victory of the proletarian revolution seemed unreal as a fairy tale, as the logic of socialist construction in the USSR clashed with incompatible private and group interests. Securing raw materials, permissions to import necessary equipment, additional food supplies, and so on—all this became a logistical nightmare and led to interdepartmental wars. To survive in this struggle and to succeed, groups and clans were formed around each influential Politburo member. In the centralized administrative system, even minor conflicts could be resolved only at the highest bureaucratic level, and each interested party played its own "administrative resource" to its fullest capacity. Many caricatures provide excellent illustrations of this mechanism.

In July 1930, the Politburo resolved to rebuild and expand the Moscow factory Serp i molot (Hammer and Sickle). However, the Supreme Economic Council and the People's Commissariat of Heavy Industry had widely diverging views on how to implement this restructuring, and the question eventually returned to the Politburo. In that conflict, the people's commissar of heavy industry, Ordzhonikidze, favored A. I. Gurevich, head of the Chief Administration of the Metallurgical Industry (fig. 151). Mezhlauk, for all his reasoning, had no chance against this political heavyweight.

Resolution of departmental conflicts of interest consumed a lot of time in the Politburo. In the fall of 1930, the Locomotive Association of the Supreme Economic Council refused to comply with the resolution to expand the tractor shop of the Kharkov locomotive plant to accommodate tank production. (Related documents refer to tanks as "road machines.") After a difficult behind-the-scenes discussion, the parties reached a compromise. The head of the Locomotive Association managed to convince the Politburo members that reorganization of the shop was inappropriate, but the latter insisted on fulfilling the military order in Kharkov. The image of "peddler" V. I. Kuritsyn selling tanks to other factories is an accurate representation of the practice of shoving aside unwelcome responsibilities (fig. 143).

The search by trial and error for new forms of centralized economic administration inevitably led to mistakes, failures to fulfill the plan, and costly accidents. In order to avoid taking political responsibility for inefficient management, the top leaders preferred to look for criminal intent as a possible explanation. The drawings often refer to wrecking and wreckers (figs. 78, 113, 149). On 10 May 1933, the Politburo held a second discussion of wrecking at the electric power stations. Krzhizhanovsky, as chairman of the Glavenergo (Chief Administration of Energy Services and Organizations), again tried to play down the frequency and the scale of accidents in his department. This earned him a place in the caricatures (fig. 148).

The worst accidents happened in railway transport. Newspapers did not report fatalities, but the leaders of the country were quite aware of the real state of affairs (figs. 153, 155). M. L. Rukhimovich, people's commissar of communications in the early 1930s, became a scapegoat for those misfortunes. On 19 September 1931 Stalin wrote from his vacation retreat: "As long as the gang of self-enamored and self-complacent bureaucrats like Rukhimovich manage the Transport, scoffing, in the Menshevik fashion, at the C[entral] C[ommittee] resolutions and spreading around corrupting skepticism, the CC resolutions will remain on the back burner."

Thus Stalin's attitude toward the chief railwayman was no secret to the Politburo members. The published caricatures directly link Rukhimovich to the accidents (figs. 154, 156). As soon as he was replaced by Kaganovich, the flow of such caricatures ceased. Transport remained a bottleneck of rapid industrialization, and its problems were regularly discussed at all levels of the party and the government. At the seventeenth party congress, one of the transport bosses, V. I. Polonsky, put on sackcloth and ashes while giving traditional explanations: "The main cause for the poor performance of the railway transport is people, their poor organization, lack of iron, conscious discipline, in the first place, among the executive staff" (fig. 166).

At the February–March 1937 plenum of the Central Committee, people's commissar of communications Kaganovich vividly expounded on the huge scale of wrecking in railway transportation. Mezhlauk's drawing provides a good illustration of the part of the report dealing with the enemies "clogging" a station with empty cars, which forced Kaganovich and the secretary of the West Siberian territorial party committee, Robert I. Eikhe, to personally "unclog" the mess (fig. 175).

Caricatures regarding economics, while simplistic, clearly demonstrate that the Bolshevik leaders ultimately failed to master efficient management. After relinquishing, in the early 1930s, market mechanisms, they relied on administrative pressure and noneconomic incentives. Departments and ministries became appanage principalities controlling various industries, and fear became the main motivation for achieving the best results. Heads of the Supreme Economic Council, Dzerzhinsky and, later, Ordzhonikidze, could only manage their subordinates heavy-handedly (fig. 152). The council itself, an ugly monster, loomed menacingly over the directors (fig. 147).

Fig. 139.
V. I. Mezhlauk, *G. K.
Ordzhonikidze and V. I. Rykov.*
Blue pencil. Inscription: "Sergo
and Rykov by the end of the
financial commission meeting."
RGASPI, f. 74, op. 2, d. 169, l. 103.

Fig. 140.
V. I. MEZHLAUK, *Give!—Take it!* Pencil. A manager demanding more investment, while the People's Commissariat of Finances and the State Planning Committee (the hands at upper left making a rude "get lost" gesture at him) refuse his demands.
RGASPI, f. 74, op. 2, d. 170, l. 129.

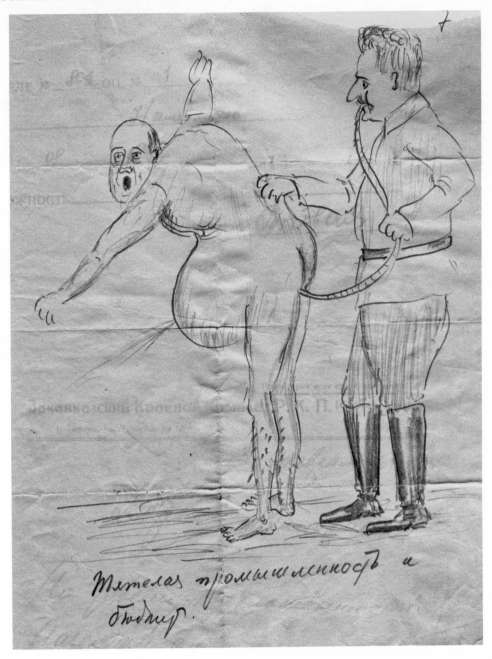

Fig. 141.
V. I. Mezhlauk, *G. K. Ordzhonikidze.* Pencil. Inscription by the artist: "Heavy industry and the budget."
RGASPI, f. 79, op. 1, d. 802, l. 7.

Fig. 142.
V. I. Mᴇᴢʜʟᴀᴜᴋ, *G. L. Piatakov.* 31 March 1932. Black and red pencil. Inscription by the artist:
"People's Commissariat of Heavy Industry and other industries. As a result of budget, capital works,
and material balance deliberations."
RGASPI, f. 74, op. 2, d. 169, l. 143.

Fig. 143.
V. I. MEZHLAUK, *V. I. Kuritsyn*.
25 October 1930. Pencil.
Inscription by the artist: "Vasia
Kuritsyn: 'Tanks! Tanks! Hot!
A prickly and dangerous
product! Who's interested?
Not fitting my factories!'"
RGASPI, f. 74, op. 2, d. 169, l. 107.

Fig. 144.
UNKNOWN ARTIST, *V. I.
Mezhlauk*. Blue ink. Inscription:
"Valery Ivanovich Comrade
Mezhlauk in distress."
RGASPI, f. 74, op. 2, d. 169, l. 32.

Fig. 145.
V. I. Mezhlauk, *L. M. Kaganovich*. Violet ink. Inscription by the artist: "Failed equilibrists,
or 'gave attention to transport, [but] fucked up the plows.'"
RGASPI, f. 74, op. 2, d. 170, l. 13.

Fig. 146.
V. I. MEZHLAUK, *Pulled out the nose, the tail got stuck.* Violet ink. Inscription by the artist: "Pulled out the nose, the tail got stuck. Piatakov: 'We pulled out tractor spare parts, but neglected the r/w [railway] spare parts.'" Inscription on top: "21 April. At the meeting of the Molotov commission on the spare parts for the People's Commissariat of Communications."

RGASPI, f. 74, op. 2, d. 170, l. 9.

Fig. 147.
V. I. MEZHLAUK, *How Kostia Ukhanov sees VSNKh USSR.* 5 January 1930. Pencil. (Konstantin Ukhanov was chairman of the Moscow provincial executive committee, 1929–32, and deputy people's commissar of supplies, 1932–34. He was shot in 1937. VSNKh stands for Supreme Council of the National Economy.)

RGASPI, f. 74, op. 2, d. 169, l. 81.

Fig. 148.
V. I. Mezhlauk, *Situation at the electric power stations.* 10 May 1933. Pencil. Lower inscription: "The same, according to Glavenergo." Inscription on the monster and the lamb: "Accident."

RGASPI, f. 74, op. 2, d. 169, l. 174.

Fig. 149.
V. I. Mezhlauk, *G. L. Piatakov and L. M. Kaganovich.* Pencil. Inscription by the artist: "Two peas in a pod. 2 deputies. 'What can you say about wrecking at the electric power stations?' 'Er, hum . . . Quality . . . NKVT [People's Commissariat of Foreign Trade] . . . ahem, ahem.'" On the reverse, inscription by the artist: "To K. Ye. Voroshilov."

RGASPI, f. 74, op. 2, d. 169, l. 160–160 rev.

Fig. 150.
V. I. Mezhlauk, *L. M. Kaganovich.* 20 February 1934. Pencil.
Inscription by the artist: "Plan fulfilled—*We have won.* NKTP. Plan
frustrated—it's not *us*, it's him." On the reverse, inscription by the
artist: *"To K. Voroshilov. Strictly personal."*
RGASPI, f. 74, op. 2, d. 170, l. 7.

Fig. 151.
V. I. Mezhlauk, *V. I. Mezhlauk, A. I. Gurevich, G. K. Ordzhonikidze.* 4 October 1930. Black ink.
Inscription by the artist: "Family scene. *Gurevich:* 'Aahh! I don't want an open-hearth furnace,
a forge, and shape casting at Serp [i molot]! I don't want! Aahh!' *Mezhlauk:* 'There, there, darling,
calm down, dear. Say, why don't you want it?' *Gurevich:* 'Just because! I don't want! Aahhh!' *Sergo
[Ordzhonikidze]:* 'What's going on? Who's bullying my boy? You, son of a bitch, eat my grandma's
pants! I'll show you!' "
RGASPI, f. 74, op. 2, d. 169, l. 106.

Fig. 152.
V. I. Mezhlauk, *F. E. Dzerzhinsky and G. K. Ordzhonikidze*. Pencil. Inscription by the artist:
"What VSNKh is doing to people. 1925, 1931."
RGASPI, f. 74, op. 2, d. 169, l. 142.

Fig. 153.
V. I. Mezhlauk, *Accident at kilometer x.* 23 December 1929. Black ink.
RGASPI, f. 74, op. 2, d. 169, l. 62.

Fig. 155.
V. I. Mezhlauk, *Also quality of products.* Black ink.
RGASPI, f. 74, op. 2, d. 169, l. 180.

Fig. 154.
V. I. Mezhlauk, *M. L. Rukhimovich.* 15 November 1930. Black ink. Inscription by the artist: "Every night, a guilty conscience reveals to the tormented people's commissar of communications dozens of killed innocents."

RGASPI, f. 74, op. 2, d. 169, l. 110.

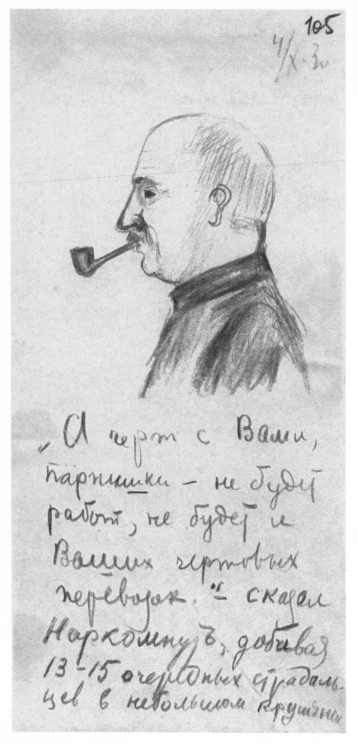

Fig. 156.
V. I. Mezhlauk, *M. L. Rukhimovich.* 4 October 1930. Blue pencil. Inscription by the artist: " 'To hell with you, guys. No works—no damned shipping operations of yours,' said the people's commissar of communications, finishing off another 13–15 poor victims of a minor crash."

RGASPI, f. 74, op. 2, d. 169, l. 105.

The Congress of the Victors and the Plenum of the Condemned

All of the drawings in the last section of the book belong to Valery Mezhlauk. They hardly can be called caricatures or lampoons: with rare exceptions, the portraits are spiritless, and the author's personality only occasionally reveals itself in inscriptions. Mezhlauk became a detached chronicler of the two highly important party forums of the mid-1930s: the seventeenth Communist Party congress and the February–March 1937 Plenum of the Central Committee.

The seventeenth party congress, dubbed "the congress of the victors," was held from 26 January to 10 February 1934. It was marked by Stalin's compromise with moderate Politburo members and public self-criticism by the oppositionists. The congress adopted the second five-year plan, and it was characterized by resounding glorification of Stalin, which set the tone for the personality cult celebrations. The February–March 1937 plenum marked the beginning of the Great Terror, with renewed attacks on enemies and the right opposition. In particular, Bukharin and Rykov were accused of plotting conspiracies and were subjected to badgering and humiliation. The plenum expelled them from the party and endorsed their arrest. If "the congress of the victors" reveled in optimism and placidity, the plenum reflected nervousness and fear, a frantic search for real and imaginary enemies, and desperate attempts to demonstrate loyalty to Stalin.

A large number of sketches made at the seventeenth congress show that Mezhlauk was bored while sitting in the presidium. His drawings changed hands, and ended up in Voroshilov's file. We arranged the portraits of orators according to the order of their presentations. Kaganovich's speech seemed to contain more figures than words (fig. 162). The chairman failed to stop Piatakov, enthusiastically defending the interests of his People's Commissariat of Heavy Industry (fig. 160). Provincial leaders reported successes. The delegate from the Trans-Caucasian Republic, G. M. Musabekov, finished his speech military-style: "Under the leadership of the Central Committee, under the leadership of the most brilliant leader, the leader of the world proletariat, Comrade Stalin, we will storm, in closed ranks, the great tasks of the second five-year plan, and we will honorably fulfill these great tasks" (fig. 161). Three years later he would join other ranks—the ones of the victims of the Great Terror.

Of the recanting oppositionists, Mezhlauk pictured only Kamenev (figs. 163, 164). At the session on 5 February 1934, Kamenev said: "If I dare, from this rostrum, to offer you this chronicle of defeats, this chronicle of mistakes and crimes, it is only because I realize, deep inside, that I have turned the page, that I have left it in the past, that it is a cadaver which I can now dissect calmly, without emotion, just as I used to dissect the political cadavers of the enemies of the working class—the Mensheviks and the Trotskyists." Labeling his differences with the party a crime, the former comrade of Lenin offered his services to dissect the still unexposed enemies. It is possible that this logic led Stalin to the idea of show trials, of which Kamenev became one of the first victims.

Victors can only be optimistic. Such is the portrait of A. I. Mikoyan, people's commissar of supplies, ready to fight the bureaucracy in his own commissariat. He is surrounded and supported by Soviet retail outlets—from supermarkets to kiosks selling refreshments (fig. 157). The youngest of the Bolshevik elite, Mikoyan ardently defended the advantages of retail stores over rationing and food cards: "Soviet retail stores are quite different. . . . Here salesmen have to maintain discipline and order, they should not engage in heated discussions with the customers, which often involves brandishing heavy objects and using strong Russian language." A short-tempered Armenian, Mikoyan is portrayed as an archetypal dzhigit, a brave Caucasian warrior.

Pictures of Mikhail Kalinin are quite different—ironic and even derisive. "The all-union elder" was known for thick peasantlike speech, and spontaneous humor, and his reports were often interrupted by laughter from the audience. Kalinin at first promised "not to ruffle any feathers," then continued by quoting the classics of Marxism, and, finally, proclaimed himself a special type of orator who does not lead the masses but only "explains and makes hints." The caricaturist had only to put these pearls of speech together (fig. 168). When Kalinin exhausted his time limit, he turned to the audience for support, and it was gladly granted (fig. 167).

The legendary former commander of the First Cavalry army, S. M. Budionny, continued to lobby for horse breeding in peacetime. He stressed that "a horse in no way can be in conflict with the development of our auto transport and other machines." It is hard to say which Mezhlauk managed to reproduce better—Budionny's fabulous mustache or the affectionate horse clinging to its devoted ally (fig. 165).

It is significant that the gallery of drawings ends with the February–March Central Committee Plenum, which ushered in mass repression. It was the artist Mezhlauk's swan song: along with the majority of attendees at the congress of the victors and many participants of the plenum, he did not survive the purges. It is important to remember, however, that almost all of the Bolshevik leaders who perished in the terror were also its creators. Many of them, imagining that they were in charge of historical changes, in fact were swept along by the flow and ended up at the dead end, together with the caricatured "enemies" that had been exposed (fig. 171).

These images show Mezhlauk as a victim of self-censorship. Caricatures of Bukharin and Rykov as swastika-marked animals were typical of the official Soviet press. Long before the revolution, Trotsky addressed his opponents by saying, "You would like to harness the timid doe of artistic satire to the wagon of a political party." The drawings in this section are good examples of such attempts.

The pictures quote speakers verbatim at the same time they reconstruct the poisonous atmosphere in the party. Speaking of the first item on the agenda (the Bukharin case), people's commissar of the interior Nikolai Yezhov declared that the rightists "have in fact created a bloc with the Trotskyists and anti-Soviet SR [socialist revolutionary] and Menshevik parties, and, together, they assumed the leadership over the anti-Soviet remnants of the defeated classes in our country, and in the end transformed into agents of fascist bourgeoisie." The drawing accompanying this statement shows a fat banker with the ubiquitous "capitalist" top hat, and the oppositionists cringing before him (fig. 169). It is interesting that the jacket of the capitalist displays an American flag, though the oppositionists were accused of working for German Nazism and Japanese militarism.

Portraits of Rykov, in which he puts himself right with his former comrades, show his fear and confusion amid the tragic farce of the Soviet inquisition (figs. 172, 173). Not yet arrested, the former head of government at the podium looks like a convict in the dock. Nikolai Bukharin also became a subject for Mezhlauk again at the plenum. Gone, however, are the placid humor and rude but friendly jokes. Bukharin, whom Lenin once called "the party's favorite," is now portrayed as Judas, guilty of all mortal sins (fig. 170). One of the accusations was that he had maintained contacts with the graduates of the Red Professors school (which he headed), many of whom had been accused of right deviations. "It is no wonder that the entire Bukharinist school is in prison. Almost all of them have confessed that they had been double-dealers, enemies—because Bukharin taught them," said Mikoyan at the plenum.

Bukharin did not deny liaisons with his students but stressed the human, nonpolitical side of it: "They often stood up for me when there were attacks that I considered unfair . . . I felt indebted to them." On the eve of the plenum, Bukharin wrote a statement refuting accusations by Karl Radek, who had already been charged and convicted at a show trial. Investigators used Radek as a source of new accusations. In his statement Bukharin named Valery Mezhlauk, among others, as his student. During the first day of the plenum, Bukharin gave an overly emotional speech in which he accurately described the situation: "When there is a particular political atmosphere, when all eyes and all fingers are pointing at me (when Radek said that I was so and so, it is Radek's index finger pointing me out to the whole world); when the matter concerns a person under investigation, especially a rightist, then he is asked 'who is your leader?,' the pointing finger, the finger of two [show] trials, Radek's finger is pointing at me."

Mezhlauk illustrated Bukharin's words with a picture of Radek pointing at the rightists from behind prison bars (fig. 171). The picture also shows Kamenev and Piatakov, who had already been executed, still "dissecting" their former comrades. And there is a group of Bukharin's students entering the prison courtyard, ready to collaborate with the investigation.

The directness and crudeness of such allusions reveal the artist's fear, and the fear of the rest of the party elite, of being accused. Further examples abound: Here is a portrait of Klavdia Nikolaeva, secretary of the Trade Union Council, praying vigorously to avoid being named a spy or a wrecker (fig. 177). S. V. Kosior and P. P. Postyshev, "Romeo and Juliet" from Ukraine, accused of insufficient vigor in rooting out the enemies in their republic, are scared and seem to foresee their fate (fig. 180). New leaders of the NKVD, the police apparatus, are recanting and confessing their mistakes. For now they have been successful in shifting the blame on the commissar of state security, G. A. Molchanov (fig. 178). During the plenum, Stalin pointedly asked Yezhov whether Molchanov had been arrested yet, and received a positive answer.

Lavrenty Beria, who replaced Yezhov as head of the NKVD in 1938, sensed the moment to attack his predecessors who, instead of educating Bolshevik cadres, encouraged "unscrupulousness, scheming, intrigues, and squabbles" (fig. 179). The people's commissar of defense industry, Rukhimovich, was not stingy with the streams of expletives he aimed at Piatakov and other arrested managers who supposedly had frustrated the construction of military factories. In order to save the industry, he made an "earnest request to the secretaries of the provincial and territorial party committees where these 'ladies' [factories] are being built to help us finish the construction in time." This loud but mysterious request did not leave Mezhlauk unmoved (fig. 176).

Fear and insecurity generated the desire to play it safe, to reinsure one's position with abundant lies and flattery. Those close to Stalin strove to guess his secret intentions in order to anticipate them. Thus, during the third show trial, Procurator General Vyshinsky referred to the accused as filthy degenerates. Those who did not demonstrate appropriate ingenuity became among those at risk themselves.

One of the drawings from the plenum deals with the speech by Nikolai Osinsky on 26 February 1937 (fig. 174). A former supporter of Bukharin in the "left" communist faction and in the newspaper *Izvestia*, Osinsky said that he was forced to speak against his will. He recalled several theoretical discussions with Bukharin, who admitted that he did not quite understand dialectics and the category of quality. Osinsky came to the conclusion that Bukharin was a bourgeois positivist. The plenum participants, however, were expecting something different. Mezhlauk's drawing reminds the "Plato" Osinsky that it was not the time to have his head in the clouds but to come down to earth and speak about the terror and the facts of high treason (Radek is pictured bringing in a fascist and an English sailor or a Japanese samurai, and Bukharin is firing at the USSR from the Far East).

The archival collection of caricatures ends with the February–March 1937 Plenum of the Central Committee. Valery Mezhlauk survived Bukharin by only a short while. He was arrested in December 1937 and shot in July 1938. Thus ended the "duel" of the two top Bolshevik caricaturists. Their drawings were added to their police files. Beria's notes on some of them show that the new NKVD chief, knowing about Voroshilov's fondness for caricatures, was sending him pictures from the Mezhlauk file. This saved some of his works, but the bulk of the cartoons from the Bolshevik Olympus vanished without a trace.

Fig. 157.
V. I. Mezhlauk, *A. I. Mikoyan.* [4 February 1934.] Pencil. Inscription by the artist: "Fight the bureaucracy in the realm of the People's Commissariat of Supplies!" On top of the picture: "17th Party Congress, February." On the reverse: "To C[omrade] Voroshilov. Personally."
RGASPI, f. 74, op. 2, d. 170, l. 5.

Fig. 158.
V. I. Mezhlauk, *A. I. Mikoyan.* [4 February 1934.] Pencil. Inscription by the artist: "We are going to finish this appetizer now, and if someone interferes, we will get him with the same weapon!" On the plate: "Theses for the 17th VKP(b) Congress."

RGASPI, f. 74, op. 2, d. 170, l. 25.

Fig. 159.
V. I. MEZHLAUK, *G. L. Piatakov.* [4 February 1934.] Pencil. Inscription by the artist: "In the second five-year period we will give everything to others. (To himself: 'Like hell we will! You can whistle for it.')"
RGASPI, f. 74, op. 2, d. 170, l. 29.

Fig. 160.
V. I. MEZHLAUK, *G. L. Piatakov, S. V. Kosior.* [4 February 1934.] Pencil. Inscription by the artist: "Chairman: 'I cannot keep this red-haired devil in check.'"
RGASPI, f. 74, op. 2, d. 170, l. 30.

Fig. 161.
V. I. Mezhlauk, *G. M. Musabekov.* [4 February 1934.] Pencil. Inscription by the artist: "C[omrade] Musabekov: 'We . . . will . . . start an of-fensive.' "

RGASPI, f. 74, op. 2, d. 170, l. 23.

Fig. 162.
V. I. Mezhlauk, *L. M. Kaganovich.* [5 February 1934.] Pencil. Inscription by the artist: "M. Kaganovich bewilders the congress with the serenity of his speech since no objections are raised."

RGASPI, f. 74, op. 2, d. 170, l. 22.

Fig. 163.
V. I. Mezhlauk, *L. B.
Kamenev.* [5 February 1934.]
Pencil. Inscription by the artist:
"Kamenev dissecting himself or
doing a hara-kiri."
RGASPI, f. 74, op. 2, d. 170, l. 32.

Fig. 164.
V. I. Mezhlauk, *L. B.
Kamenev.* [5 February 1934.]
Pencil. Inscription by the artist:
"17th congress. F[ebruary] 1934.
C[omrade] Kamenev dissecting
himself."
RGASPI, f. 74, op. 2, d. 170, l. 4.

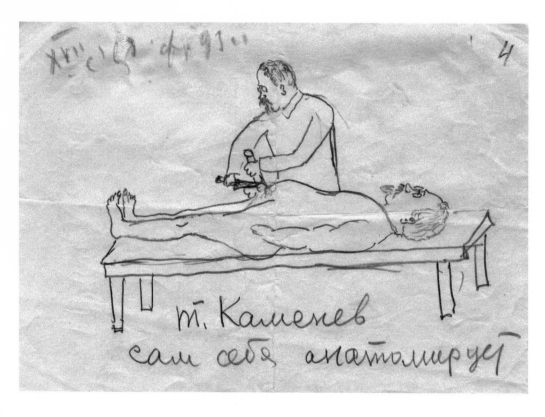

Fig. 165.
V. I. Mezhlauk, *S. M. Budionny*. [5 February 1934.] Pencil.
Inscription by the artist: "A benefactor and utterly devoted
defender of the horse."

RGASPI, f. 74, op. 2, d. 170, l. 28.

Fig. 166.
V. I. Mezhlauk, *V. I. Polonsky*.
[7 February 1934.] Pencil.
Inscription by the artist:
" '[A thief has] a hat on fire'
[Russian idiom meaning a guilty
person cannot hide his guilt].
C[omrade] Polonsky: 'And that's
what executive staff discipline is
like in transport!' "

RGASPI, f. 74, op. 2, d. 170, l. 26.

Fig. 167.
V. I. Mezhlauk, *M. I. Kalinin.* [7 February 1934.] Pencil.
Inscription by the artist: " 'Please, please [talk']'?! I'm gonna give
you a thrashing, you pompadours! I'll show you 'please talk'!"
The cover of the book reads "K. Marx and F. Engels."
RGASPI, f. 74, op. 2, d. 170, l. 24.

Fig. 168.
V. I. Mezhlauk, *M. I. Kalinin.*
[7 February 1934.] Pencil.
Inscription by the artist: "Due
to my social position, I do not
lead but only explain so as to
avoid ruffling any feathers [in
Russian, 'to tease the geese']."
The volume under his arm reads
"K. Marx and F. Engels."
RGASPI, f. 74, op. 2, d. 170, l. 31.

Fig. 169.
V. I. Mezhlauk, *L. D. Trotsky, N. I. Bukharin, A. I. Rykov.* [February 1937.] Pencil. Inscription by the artist: Trotsky: "Your might is indestructible, O capitalism of the USA! Forgive me my trespasses and give me my daily bread!" "Rykov to Bukharin: 'That will do for you! Let me lick, too!'" On top, inscription by Stalin in blue pencil: "Capitalism." On the reverse, inscription by Beria: "To Comrade Anastas [Mikoyan]. I am sending a drawing by C[omrade] V[alery] Mezhlauk. L[avrenty] Beria."
RGASPI, f. 74, op. 2, d. 170, l. 77–77 rev.

Fig. 170.
V. I. Mezhlauk, *N. I. Bukharin.* [February 1937.] Pencil. Inscription by the artist: "'Holy fool' Bukharin Iscariotsky." On the reverse, inscription by Beria: "To Comrade Zhdanov."
RGASPI, f. 74, op. 2, d. 170, l. 92–92 rev.

Fig. 171.
V. I. Mezhlauk, *At the dead end.* [February 1937.] Pencil. On the banner above the entering crowd: "Bukharin's school." On the left, risen from the dead and pointing fingers, are Kamenev and Piatakov. Bottom: "At the dead end." On the reverse, inscription by Beria: "To Comrade Zhdanov. Drawing by C[omrade] V. Mezhlauk. L. Beria."

RGASPI, f. 74, op. 2, d. 170, l. 123–123 rev.

Fig. 172.
V. I. Mezhlauk, *A. I. Rykov.* [24 February 1937.] Pencil. Inscription by the artist: "'When Radin told me to remove the leadership I didn't understand him (it was before the Zinovievite-Trotskyist trial), and even asked—how shall we decorate it, with flowers, ribbons, or laurel leaves?' The touching naïveté of the little baby Alesha [Rykov]." (In Russian, the word *ubrat'* means both "to remove" and "to decorate.") On the reverse, inscription by Beria: "To Comrade Voroshilov. Drawing by V. Mezhlauk. L. B[eria]."

RGASPI, f. 74, op. 2, d. 170, l. 122–122 rev.

Fig. 173.
V. I. Mezhlauk, A. A.
Andreyev, A. I. Rykov.
[24 February 1937.] Pencil.
Inscription by the artist:
"Comrade Andreyev's
summary: 'Well, you are a
shitty fibber!'" On the reverse,
inscription by Beria: "To
Comrade Andreyev. Drawing
by V. Mezhlauk. L. B[eria]."
RGASPI, f. 74, op. 2, d. 170, l. 121–121 rev.

Fig. 174.
V. I. Mezhlauk, N. *Osinsky (V. V. Obolensky).* [26 February 1937.]
Pencil. Inscriptions by the artist: "C[omrade] Osinsky according
to Plato." Upper left: "Mysterious phenomenon of Radek." Upper
right: "Phenomenon of Bukharin. 'What is dialectics and quality?'"
Lower left: "Noumenon of Radek." Lower right: "Noumenon of
Bukharin." Bottom: "Sinful Earth." On the reverse, inscription by
Beria: "To Comrade Zhdanov. Drawing by C[omrade]
V. Mezhlauk, upon request. L. Beria."
RGASPI, f. 74, op. 2, d. 170, l. 88.

Fig. 175.
V. I. MEZHLAUK, L. M.
Kaganovich, R. I. Eikhe.
[28 February 1937.] Pencil.
Inscription by the artist:
"Comrade Kaganovich
reported: 'Comrade Eikhe
clogged and unclogged the
[railway] junctures with us,
until we started unclogging the
Eikhe [station] itself.'" On the
reverse, inscription by Beria:
"Klim [Voroshilov]! I am
sending a drawing by
V. Mezhlauk. L. Beria."

RGASPI, f. 74, op. 2, d. 170, l. 91–91 rev.

Fig. 176.
V. I. MEZHLAUK, M. L.
Rukhimovich. 1 March 1937.
Pencil. Inscription by the artist:
"'Comrades, there is no war
without g-gunp-powder. We
have discussed it a long time
ago in the waiting room and
decided: let every provincial
party committee secretary take
one of our ladies [military
factories]!' Loud but puzzling.
Rukhimovich at the Plenum,
1 March [19]37." On the
reverse, inscription by Beria:
"Klim [Voroshilov]! I am
sending a drawing by
C[omrade] V. Mezhlauk.
L. Beria."

RGASPI, f. 74, op. 2, d. 170, l. 86–86 rev.

Fig. 177.
V. I. Mezhlauk, *K. I. Nikolaeva.* [February–March 1937.] Pencil. Inscription by the artist: "Kl[avdia] Nikolaeva: 'Oh God almighty, what's going on, what's going on! Let this cup pass from me!'" On the reverse, inscription by Beria: "To Comrade V. M. Molotov. Drawing by V. Mezhlauk. L. Beria."
RGASPI, f. 74, op. 2, d. 170, l. 90–90 rev.

Fig. 178.
V. I. MEZHLAUK, *Ya. S. Agranov and L. M. Zakovsky.* 3 March 1937. Pencil. Inscription by the artist: "Certainly, we are at fault. But we remained silent, and Molchanov spoke out." (The name Molchanov is derived from the Russian word for silence.)

RGASPI, f. 74, op. 2, d. 170, l. 54.

Fig. 179.
V. I. MEZHLAUK, *L. P. Beria.*
[4 March 1937.] Pencil.
Inscription by the artist: " 'I cannot but point out the sad role played in the preparation of our cadres by comrades M. Orakhelashvili, Krinitsky, Kakhiani, Eliava, Kartvelishvili.' The thief's hat is on fire, or the subversion by C[omrade] Beria." On the reverse: "*To C[omrade] Zhdanov.* I am sending excerpts from Comrade Beria's speech as recorded by Comrade Mezhlauk. D. Bagirov."

RGASPI, f. 74, op. 2, d. 170, l. 85–85 rev.

Fig. 180.
V. I. Mᴇᴢʜʟᴀᴜᴋ, *S. V. Kosior and P. P. Postyshev.* [3 March 1937.] Pencil. Inscription by the artist: "For never was a story of more woe than this of Juliet and her Romeo (in this case, Ukrainian)." Inscription by Beria: "To Comrade Kaganovich. I am sending a drawing by V. Mezhlauk. L. Beria."
RGASPI, f. 74, op. 2, d. 170, l. 78.

Fig. 181.
V. I. Mezhlauk, *I. D. Kabakov, S. V. Kosior, A. A. Andreyev.* [February–March 1937.] Pencil. Inscription by the artist: "C[omrade] Kosior: 'I am asking for permission to speak.' C[omrade] Andreyev: 'Eh?! Who is it? Where is he?' C[omrade] Kabakov: 'Let him say a word, for a holiday's sake, don't interfere.'" On the reverse, inscription by Beria: "To Comrade Mikoyan. I am sending a drawing by V. Mezhlauk. L. Beria."

RGASPI, f. 74, op. 2, d. 170, l. 87–87 rev.

Drawings by Artist

The drawings are indexed here according to their figure numbers

M. L. Belotsky: 105, 106.

N. I. Bukharin: 1, 2, 4, 5, 7, 9, 10, 13, 15, 19, 28, 31, 34, 39, 42, 46, 64, 65, 68, 69, 98, 103, 138.

G. M. Krzhizhanovsky: 104.

V. I. Mezhlauk: 8, 12, 18, 23, 24, 25, 27, 30, 35, 38, 40, 41, 43, 45, 47, 50, 53, 54, 55, 56, 59, 61, 62, 73, 74, 75, 77, 78, 79, 81, 82, 92, 95, 96, 97, 99, 100, 107, 108, 109, 110, 111, 112, 113, 114, 116, 117, 121, 123, 124, 125, 126, 127, 128, 129, 130, 131, 132, 133, 134, 135, 136, 137, 139, 140, 141, 142, 143, 145, 146, 147, 148, 149, 150, 151, 152, 153, 154, 155, 156, 157, 158, 159, 160, 161, 162, 163, 164, 165, 166, 167, 168, 169, 170, 171, 172, 173, 174, 175, 176, 177, 178, 179, 180, 181.

K. Radek: 101.

I. V. Stalin: 63.

Ye. M. Yaroslavsky: 6, 14, 16, 20, 21, 22, 26, 29, 32, 33, 36, 37, 44, 48, 51, 52, 57, 58, 70, 71, 72, 80, 83, 85, 86, 87, 88, 91, 93, 94.

Unattributed: 3, 11, 17, 49, 60, 66, 67, 76, 84, 89, 90, 102, 115, 118, 119, 120, 122, 144.

ANNALS OF COMMUNISM

Each volume in the series Annals of Communism will publish selected and previously inaccessible documents from former Soviet state and party archives in a narrative that develops a particular topic in the history of Soviet and international communism. Separate English and Russian editions will be prepared. Russian and Western scholars work together to prepare the documents for each volume. Documents are chosen not for their support of any single interpretation but for their particular historical importance or their general value in deepening understanding and facilitating discussion. The volumes are designed to be useful to students, scholars, and interested general readers.

Yale University Press gratefully acknowledges the financial support given for this publication by the Daphne Seybolt Culpeper Foundation, the David Woods Kemper Memorial Foundation, Joseph W. Donner, the Edward H. Andrews Foundation, the Historical Research Foundation, the Lynde and Harry Bradley Foundation, Jeremiah Milbank, Roger Milliken, the Milton V. Brown Foundation, Lloyd H. Smith, the William H. Donner Foundation, and Keith Young.